THE SANTIAGO
PILGRIMAGE

Also by Jean-Christophe Rufin in English translation

The Abyssinian

The Siege of Isfahan

Brazil Red

The Red Collar

The Dream Maker

Jean-Christophe Rufin

THE SANTIAGO
PILGRIMAGE

WALKING THE IMMORTAL WAY

Translated from the French by
Martina Dervis and Malcolm Imrie

MACLEHOSE PRESS
QUERCUS · LONDON

First published in the French language as
Immortelle randonnée: Compostelle malgré moi by
Éditions Guérin, Chamonix, in 2013
First published in Great Britain in 2016 by

MacLehose Press
An imprint of Quercus Publishing Ltd
Carmelite House
50 Victoria Embankment
London EC4Y 0DZ

An Hachette UK company

INSTITUT
FRANÇAIS
ROYAUME-UNI

This book is supported by the Institute Français (Royaume Uni)
as part of the Burgess programme

ISBN (HB) 978 0 85705 998 7
ISBN (Ebook) 978 1 84866 779 2

10 9 8 7 6 5 4 3 2 1

Designed and typeset in Quadraat by Libanus Press, Marlborough
Printed and bound in Great Britain by Clays Ltd, St Ives plc

CONTENTS

1	The Organisation	7
2	Starting Point	13
3	Why?	18
4	Love on the Road	23
5	Setting Off	31
6	A Savage in the City	38
7	First Wild Camp	43
8	Fortunes and Misfortunes of the Pilgrim Camper	49
9	Solitudes	53
10	Vespers in Zenarruza	59
11	Marathon and Santiago, One Struggle!	67
12	Bilbao	74
13	On the Ferries of Cantabria	84
14	The Pipeline God	91
15	Beauty Defiled	97
16	In the Guru's Lair	103
17	Farewell to the Coast	110
18	Cantabria: The School of Frugality	115
19	In the Camino Alembic	120
20	Ancient Asturias	128
21	Bacchus and Saint Paul	134
22	A Big Slice of Christianity	141
23	In the Tracks of Alfonso II and Buddha	148
24	Encounters	156
25	At the Summit of the Way	168

26 An Apparition in a Forest   180
27 Galicia! Galicia!   185
28 Roman Night   195
29 Losing the Way   203
30 The French Way   210
31 Final Trials   218
32 Arrival   225

I

The Organisation

If, like me, you know nothing about Santiago de Compostela before setting off, you probably imagine an ancient path winding through meadows, worn over many centuries by the feet of solitary pilgrims. And you'll be completely wrong, as you'll quickly discover when you go to get the famous *credencial*, the pilgrim's passport, an essential document if you want to stay in one of the hostels en route.

You will learn that the Camino de Santiago, the Way of Saint James (or just "the Way") as it is known in English, is the object if not of a cult, then at least of an obsession, shared by many of those who have made the pilgrimage. Behind the path to Santiago de Compostela is concealed a whole, elaborate organisation: clubs and publications, guides, all kinds of specialist services. The road is a network, a brotherhood, an international. No-one is forced to join this organisation but you are made aware of it right from the start, when you receive your *credencial*, which is a lot more than a quaint piece of stiff folded paper. Once you have been duly registered as a future-former pilgrim you will be sent news about the latest scholarly research, invitations to walks and even, in some places, to evenings known as "le vin du pèlerin", where you can reminisce with other recent pilgrims over a glass or two.

I discovered this world one rainy afternoon when I went into the little shop that serves as the headquarters of the Association of Friends of Saint James, on rue des Canettes in the Saint-Sulpice neighbourhood of Paris. It looked a bit out of place among all the fashionable bars and designer shops. Reminiscent of a church hall, full of dusty clutter, it had that special atmosphere I always associate with places where community groups gather. The member of staff who welcomed me was an elderly man – today one would say "senior", but such a word has no place in the pilgrim's vocabulary. There was no-one else in the shop, and had he not immediately done his very best to appear busy I might have wondered whether I had woken him up from a nap. No sign of computers here yet; this was still the realm of yellowing index cards, stencilled leaf-lets, the overinked rubber stamp and its pad with metal case.

I felt a bit awkward declaring my intention – not yet defin-ite, so I thought – to set off on the Way. It seemed like going to confession and I feared I might have to explain myself, give a reason for wanting to make the pilgrimage. So I tried to take the initiative and blurted out a few justifications, which didn't sound at all convincing. The man just smiled and returned to practical matters: surname, first name, date of birth.

Bit by bit he led up to the big question: did I want membership of the Association *with* the newsletter – which cost more – or *without*, paying just the basic fee. He gave the price for each option. The few euros' difference seemed to him so important that he embarked on a lengthy explanation of the precise terms of each subscription. I put this down to a laudable belief in social inclusion: the poorest should not be denied their place on the Way. Later, on my walk, I discovered it was nothing of the sort: it was because pilgrims spent much of their time trying not to pay. This was not usually from necessity but rather a game, a sign of belonging to the club. I have seen walkers, and quite wealthy ones at that, doing endless sums before deciding whether to order one sandwich (for four) in a bar or walk another three kilometres in the hope of finding a cheaper one in a bakery. The pilgrims of Saint James, called *Jacquets* in French, are not always poor, far from it, but they behave as if they were. One might connect this behaviour with the first of the three vows which, along with chastity and obedience, has marked entry to monastic life since the Middle Ages; one could also, more simply, call it stinginess.

Either way, once you have your *credencial* you are asked to respect this approach and to follow it: whether or not you are on the path to God (that is your own business), you should always count the pennies.

Of course you will also meet many people who arrange an extremely comfortable pilgrimage for themselves, moving from hotel to hotel in luxury coaches and accommodating taxis. The Jacquets tend to say sanctimoniously that "Each follows the path in his own way". But it soon becomes obvious that behind this display of tolerance lies the unshakeable contempt of the "real" pilgrim for the "fake" one. The real pilgrim spends as little as possible. Now, of course it may happen that these real pilgrims – because they're ill or the hostels are full – have no alternative but to stay in a hotel (a cheap one if possible), alongside luxury travellers. But even then they will be sure to display their difference, for example by eating all the sweets incautiously left in a bowl at reception.

Still unaware of these customs, I made my first faux pas: I regally chose membership with the newsletter and, to make matters worse, let it be known that three euros more wasn't a big deal.

The man thanked me on behalf of the Association but his tight smile made it all too clear that he felt rather sorry for me. "Forgive him, Lord, for he knows not (yet) what he does."

The credencial issued by the Association of Friends of Saint James is a piece of stiff, yellowish paper folded up like a concertina. To be honest, the future-supposed pilgrim wasn't very impressed and had a little chuckle as he made his way home. On paper that had probably been recycled three times, with its big squares ready to be stamped at every stage of the journey, it really didn't look very serious. But in fact, like everything else, the credencial only reveals its true value on the Way.

When you've shoved it in your rucksack a hundred times, when you've pulled it out, soaked from a downpour, and can't find a radiator to dry it on, when you are afraid you've lost it and start searching feverishly under the suspicious eyes of a *hospitalero*, when, after an exhausting leg of the journey, you have victoriously placed it on the desk of an employee in the tourist office who, with an air of disgust, barely touches it with his official stamp, clearly concerned that the stamp might get dirty, when, having arrived in Santiago de Compostela, you proudly unfold it before the representative of the town hall so that he can draw up in Latin your pilgrimage certificate . . . then you can measure the value of this holy relic. When you are back home, the *credencial* will be one of the surviving objects from the Way which bears the marks of the ordeal.

Although the comparison is entirely worthless, I'd say that my creased, stained, sun-bleached *credencial* reminds me of the bits of paper my grandfather brought back from Buchenwald: coupons for food or the infirmary, those must have been of immense value to the deportee, and I can imagine how carefully he preserved them.

What makes the Camino de Santiago different is that it is not a punishment but a voluntary ordeal. At least, that is what you think, though this view will be swiftly challenged by experience. Anyone who walks the Camino will sooner or later end up thinking they were condemned to it. The fact that they condemned themselves alters nothing; the punishments we impose on ourselves are often no less rigorous than those society inflicts. You set off for Santiago thinking you'll find freedom, and soon, like everyone else, you discover you're just another Camino convict. Filthy, exhausted, forced to carry your burdens in all weathers, you know the simple joys of brotherhood in the same way that prisoners do. How many times, sitting on the ground outside a hostel with other down-and-outs, rubbing my painful feet, eating some evil-smelling and meagre meal, for which I paid ridiculously little, haughtily ignored by normal, free, well-dressed, well-shod passers-by, did I feel like a *zek* out of Solzhenitsyn, one of the forced labourers of the Way, known as pilgrims?

This is what the *credencial* condemns you to. And when you get home again you'll remember, in amazement, that you actually paid to get it.

2

Starting Point

We need to be clear what we're talking about here. The "real" *credencial*, in my opinion and that of those pilgrims who consider themselves worthy of the name, is a document issued in your place of residence, which accompanies you on a long journey. However, you quickly discover that at every stage of the route right up to the last, it is possible to acquire exactly the same document. Authentic pilgrims regard those who only walk the last few kilometres and then have the nerve to get themselves a *credencial* as imposters. As if this pedestrian tourism lasting a few short days was comparable to the endless treks of pilgrims who set off from France or elsewhere in Europe! There is a degree of snobbery in this reaction. Still, as you progress along the Way you gradually understand that there is also some truth in it. It has to be admitted that time plays an essential role in shaping the "real" walker.

The Camino is time's alchemy on the soul.

It is a transformation that does not happen immediately, or even quickly. The pilgrims who trudge along for week after week come to realise this. Beyond the somewhat childish pride they may feel at having made a considerable effort compared to those who only walk for a week or so, they perceive a deeper and more humble truth: a short walk is not enough to shrug off old habits. It does not radically change a person. We remain rough stone, and for this stone to be carved it requires a more protracted effort; more cold, more mud, more hunger and less sleep. That is why what matters on the Way is not where you arrive, which is the same for everyone, but where you start. It is this which determines the subtle hierarchy that exists among pilgrims. When two walkers meet, they don't ask each other "Where are you going?" because the answer is obvious, nor "Who are you?" because on the Way you are just another poor Jacquet. The question they ask is "Where did you start?" And the answer tells them right away who they're dealing with.

If the pilgrim has picked a departure point a hundred kilometres from the cathedral of Santiago de Compostela, then you probably have a simple certificate-hunter: this is the minimum distance required to obtain the famous compostela in Latin, certifying that you have made the pilgrimage. Those who acquire this mark of distinction with the minimum effort attract barely disguised mockery from "real" pilgrims. In practice, only those who have followed one of the long Spanish routes starting in the Pyrenees see themselves as members of the brotherhood of walkers. Saint-Jean-Pied-de-Port, Hendaye,

Somport – these are all honourable starting points. Setting off from Oviedo is also acceptable, for historical reasons. Although it is a lot shorter, the *Camino Primitivo* that begins at the capital of Asturias is respected for two reasons: it runs across high mountains, so the pilgrim has to cope with greater differences in altitudes and, above all, it is the original route, the one taken by King Alfonso in the ninth century, when he went to see the remains of Saint James that a monk had just discovered.

The vast majority of pilgrims take these classic routes, either the *Primitivo* or those that start at the French border. But you find a few who have come much further. They don't look especially rugged. Indeed, some frankly appear to be struggling. One might almost feel they had a delicate constitution. And they know how to add to the effect. To the question: "Where have you come from?" confidently asked by a pilgrim sure of his own achievement, since he has started out in the foothills of the Pyrenees, they will pretend to hesitate, lower their eyes modestly and say "Le Puy" or "Vézelay". These claims to glory will be followed by a silence. If those present were wearing hats, they would doff them in respect. Once these exceptional pilgrims have delivered this first uppercut, they will usually add a figure, as the knockout: "One hundred and thirty-two days", they announce. This is how long they have been putting one foot in front of the other, morning after morning.

I walked for a while with a young student who had begun his journey at Namur in Belgium. He carried a huge rucksack, full of all kinds of useless things that he had gathered as souvenirs en route. I encountered Australian women who had come from Arles, and one German who had started out in Cologne.

On a ferry across one of the *rias* on the coast of Cantabria I met a man from Haute-Savoie who had set off from his home in Marignier, just outside Geneva. I kept bumping into him after that. He wasn't a great walker. In fact he had a rather lop-sided gait, and often got lost. But whatever he did, for me he was now on a pedestal, looking down from his two thousand kilometres.

Apparently some pilgrims come from even further away. I never met any of them and I don't think many people have been lucky enough to cross their path. They are mythical creatures, part of the legends of the Way – of which there is no shortage – whose stories pilgrims share in hushed voices. Having walked from Scandinavia, Russia, the Holy Land, they are wondrous chimeras. Confined at its end by Santiago de Compostela, the pilgrimage, thanks to them, has limitless beginnings. On pilgrimage maps, you can see all these paths flowing down towards the funnel of the Pyrenees and thence to Spain. Rippling across the surface of Europe, they are the stuff of dreams.

But the starting point isn't everything because there are

still ways to cheat. The most common consists of doing the Camino one bit at a time. So it is that you sometimes meet walkers who, during the ritual of introductions, take out a big map: Vézelay, Arles or Paris. Suspicion arises if they look peculiarly fresh and clean considering the hundreds of kilometres they claim to have walked. To get the truth, you only need to ask the killer question: "Did you come all the way from . . . in one go?" At which point the boaster will lower his head and confess that he has set himself ten years to complete the journey, in one-week stages. And in fact he started yesterday. "We all follow the path in our own way." Sure, but you don't have to take us for a ride.

3

Why?

Why?

That is the obvious question people ask themselves, even when they don't ask you directly.

Back home, whenever you utter the sentence "I walked to Santiago de Compostela", you will notice the same expression on people's faces. At first, astonishment ("What was he trying to find there?"), then, as they look at you out of the corner of their eyes, suspicion.

They are drawing an obvious conclusion: "This guy must have a problem." You start feeling uncomfortable. Fortunately, we live in a world where tolerance is a virtue: the questioners quickly pull themselves together. They assume an expression of happy surprise and keen interest. "How lucky you are!" And they add – since if you are going to lie it is best to do so with wholehearted conviction: "I have always dreamt of doing that one day. . ."

The question "why?" usually ends there. By confessing that they nurture the same ambition as you, your questioners absolve you, and themselves, of any need to discuss the reasons which might lead a normal adult to walk nearly a thousand kilometres with a rucksack on his back. Then you can move straight on to "how?"

"Did you go on your own? Which places did you pass through? How long did it take?"

It is just as well that it goes like this. Because on the rare occasions where someone has asked me straight out "*Why* did you go to Santiago?", I have found it very hard to reply. This was not a sign of embarrassment but of profound perplexity.

Instead of admitting your confusion, the best solution is to offer a few leads, making them up if necessary, to distract the curiosity of your interrogators and send them off on false trails: "There were scallop shells carved on monuments in the town where I grew up" (Freudian trail). "I have always been fascinated by the world's great pilgrimages" (ecumenical trail). "I love the Middle Ages" (historical trail). "I wanted to keep walking into the sunset until I found the sea" (mystical trail).

"I needed space to think." This last answer is the one most people expect, to the point where it is considered to be the "correct" response. But it isn't self-evident. If you want to think, wouldn't it be better to stay at home, lie around in bed or in an armchair, or, at a push, to go for a short stroll somewhere near and familiar?

How do you explain to people who have never experienced it that the Way has the effect if not the virtue of making you forget the reasons that led you to it? For the confusion and multitude of thoughts that drove you to take to the road, it substitutes the simple fact of walking. You have set off, that's it. That is how it deals with the problem of why: by forgetting. You no longer know what was there before. Like those discoveries that eliminate all that preceded them, the pilgrimage to Santiago de Compostela, in its tyrannical, totalitarian way, banishes the thoughts which led you to make it.

You have already grasped the true nature of the Way. It is not easy-going as those who have not surrendered to it believe. It is a force. It insists, it takes hold of you, it assaults you, it shapes you. It does not let you speak, it silences you. Indeed, the majority of pilgrims are quite sure that they did not decide anything for themselves, but that things "happened to them". They did not take the Way, the Way took them. I am aware that such words sound deeply suspect to those who have not had this experience. Before I set off I would have shrugged my shoulders at statements like this. They smack of religious sects. They outrage reason.

Yet I quickly discovered they were accurate. On every occasion where a decision needed to be taken, I felt the Way's power winning me over, or rather, taking me over.

At the outset, I had simply decided to go on a very long walk on my own. I saw it as a sporting challenge, a means of losing a few kilos, a way of getting ready for the winter season in the mountains, a mental detox before starting to write a new book, a return to the humility needed after a period dominated by official functions and awards . . . All those things, not just one of them. I hadn't thought about following the Way of Saint James in particular. It was merely one option among many that I was mulling over, or at least so I thought. I was still at the stage where you dream over books and stories, or look at photos and internet sites. I believed I was free to choose, sovereign. What happened next showed me I was wrong.

I gradually narrowed down my choices until only two options remained: the Haute Route Pyrénées (Pyrenees High Level Route) and one of the pilgrim routes, the North Way or *Camino del Norte*. Both began at the same place: Hendaye. So it was possible to postpone the decision. Indeed I could at a pinch leave it until the last minute, once I'd got there. I assembled a kit that would be suitable for both routes. The High Level Route goes across the Pyrenean massif from west to east. There are several possible variants: sticking to paths or "off-trail". It takes about forty days. It is more mountainous and wilder than the Camino. So I prepared myself for a long hike with almost complete self-sufficiency in cold temperatures. If you can do more you can do less: if I finally chose the Way of St James I would just need to jettison some bits of high-mountain kit and I'd be ready to go. I thought I was rather smart and I had, it seemed to me, kept the choice open to the end.

External pretexts allowed me to give my final decision a semblance of rationality: at the last moment, the High Level

Route turned out to be impractical because "it was too early in the season and some sections of the route might be tricky, etc." I chose the Way of St James. The truth is, when I think about it, that I was only surrendering to a mysterious and ever stronger attraction. Of course I could rationalise it, there had never really been any question of my choosing anything else. The various plans were just an illusion, a convenient way of hiding disagreeable evidence: in reality, I had no choice. The Saint James virus had taken a deep hold on me. I do not know how I caught it. But after a silent incubation period, the malady had broken out and I had all the symptoms.

4

Love on the Road

How do you choose your starting point? There are two great philosophies, which La Palice in one his celebrated *lapalissades* might explain like this: either you leave from where you are, or from somewhere else. The choice is a more serious matter than it seems, and several pilgrims have admitted to me that they found it tough. The ideal (so it seems, for it isn't mine) is to follow the example of the man from Haute-Savoie I mentioned earlier: leave your house, hug your wife and children, pat the dog that's wagging its tail because it wants to come with you, shut the garden gate and start walking.

Those who cannot do this – because they live too far away or don't have enough time – must get closer to their goal, start as near to Spain as they can, shorten the journey to suit them. They won't set off from home, but from where then? There are many roads, and innumerable departure points. It is a difficult choice. It depends on various objective factors: the time you can spare, the places you would like to visit, the guidebooks you have bought, the stories friends have told you. But more subtle and sometimes less respectable considerations come into play.

I had better mention straight away something that readers will discover sooner or later and that should not surprise them any more than it did me: the Way is a place for encounters, not to say pickups. This aspect influences a lot of pilgrims, especially when it comes to choosing their departure point. Once again, we need to be clear about what romantic need the pilgrimage is answering. The fact is that there are several different emotional approaches to the Way.

The first is found in people who have only recently met but have already found their soulmate. Young lovers, sweethearts and fiancés fall into this category. They are often very young: lovebirds in Nike trainers and perfect health, wearing headphones. For them, it is a matter of the final push, the one that will lead them to the altar, the registry office, or at least to rocking the cradle. Walking the Way gently unites them. Hand in hand they stroll along the main roads and, when a lorry passes, a sweet shiver runs down their spines, bringing the infatuated pilgrims even closer together. They go from church to church along this holy path and – so hopes the more passionate of the two – this might well give the hint to the other. On some evenings in certain monasteries a merry saraband mingles wild laughter and bare flesh in the washrooms. The monks, who know all about this, make sure they stay mixed. On the camp beds there's much whispering and billing and cooing, and since there's no comfortable way of going any further, vows of eternal love and fidelity are exchanged.

For lovers like this, the Way is useful but it should not go on too long. After a few days, these couples, who tend to go around in groups, may start to find their attention wandering. The fiancé is tempted to look at another cleavage instead of his beloved's. As for the young woman, conquered after a hard-won struggle, she may well make comparisons from which the one who has led her this far does not emerge victorious. Thus these couples save their efforts for the final kilometres. They only walk through the very last stages. You find them in large numbers on the paths of Galicia. Like those birds that show the navigator that land is not far off, they are a sign for the pilgrim that he has nearly reached Santiago de Compostela.

It is very different for the second category, walkers who are seeking love but have not yet found it. These tend to be older: they have known life, sometimes passion and even marriage. Then happiness falls apart, and they must start all over again. At some time or another, the Way seems like the answer. Less disembodied than internet dating sites, it brings them into contact with real people, flesh and blood and sweat. Fatigue from walking softens hearts. Thirst and blisters bring people together, offering an opportunity to lavish or receive care.

Men and women who find no pity in the cities, with their cruel competitiveness and their tyrannical role models which condemn the fat, the thin, the old, the ugly, the poor, the unemployed, discover in the condition of the pilgrim an equality that gives everyone a chance.

These people, and all the more so because nature has not favoured them, prefer to set off from far away, to increase their chances. You find them scattered over hundreds of kilometres. You can watch love's halt and lame approach each other, check each other out, move apart or come together. You see them falter or fail, or sometimes cruelly spurn the offer of another's heart because the attraction is not mutual. You see disillusion, when the one who could have been the long-sought great love finally confesses, as he walks up a hill, that he is married and loves his wife. But you also see true couples forming and you hope they will be happy.

Women frequently set off in groups, no doubt to give themselves courage. I have met some who have travelled together very far, right across France, without, alas, finding the men they were hoping for. They bravely take on Spain and often, a bit further on, one of them will disappear. She has joined another group and is trying her chances with a new Prince Charming. Watching these scenes, I stupidly think of the expression "finding the right match". The Way is hard, but it sometimes has the kindness to fulfil the most secret wishes. You must know how to persevere. There is a story about an accordionist who earned his living on the Way by playing his instrument at every stopping point. He had just got divorced, he was very unhappy, and I imagine he played sad love songs, without any great success with the women he encountered. Once he had reached Santiago de Compostela, he joined a group of musicians. There he met a German woman who shared his passion for music and his wounded soul. They got married, and every year they come back to the Way together. And the joyful music they now play is a delight to hear. The story is surely too good to be true, but it is legends like this that keep faith alive in those who trust in the Way to heal their sadness.

The third category, not so romantic but no less touching, is composed of those who knew love a long time ago, entered into the sacred bonds of matrimony, and then suffered its trials and tribulations until their greatest wish was to be free again. But the freedom they seek is of the kind and considerate sort – they don't want to break up happy families or hurt anyone, they just want a bit of a breather, with a little help from Saint James.

The man at the Association of Friends of Saint James who welcomed me in Paris and gave me my *credencial* belonged to this category. When I asked him to tell me about his own pilgrimage, he did so with tears in his eyes. Despite his advanced years, he had stood up very well to the effort of walking. He found his newly acquired freedom so intoxicating that having arrived in Santiago de Compostela he didn't stop! He went straight on along a path that led down to Portugal, and if there had been a bridge spanning the waters of the Atlantic all the way to Brazil, he'd probably have crossed that too, without a second thought. The unhappy man recalled this burst of madness with a nostalgic smile. When I asked him how it all ended, he frowned. It seems that his wife had to catch a plane, a train and two buses to find him and bring him back home. But he had found freedom and had no intention of giving it up. He set off once more the next year and still dreams of doing it again.

He questioned me about my intentions. Where was I going to start? I hadn't thought about it then. Not belonging to any of the categories above I had no emotional considerations to guide my choice. I wanted to walk, that was all. I confessed that I planned to set off from Hendaye because of my reservations about the great trek across the Pyrenees. He looked at me mockingly.

"You will do what you want," he said.

This antiphrasis hid his deep certainty – and mine, too, today – that with the Way you never do what you want. You can argue, you can make other plans, but it will always win. And that is what happened.

The man from the Association had brushed aside my doubts but retained one word: Hendaye.

"If you set off from Hendaye you will take the North Way."

There are two main routes to Santiago de Compostela, both starting at the French border. The first is called the *Camino Francés*, the French Way: apart from the section crossing the Pyrenees at Roncevaux, it presents hardly any difficulties, and it is by far the most popular. On some days, one hundred and fifty pilgrims set off at the same time from Saint-Jean-Pied-de-Port . . .

The other is the coastal route, known as the *Camino del Norte*, the North Way. It is reputed to be less clearly marked, and more difficult. It starts from the French Basque country and goes through the coastal towns of San Sebastián, Bilbao and Santander.

"The North Way . . .", I mumbled. "Yes, that was my plan. What do you think? Have you done it?"

The man rummaged in a dusty cupboard and brought out a little bundle of roneoed pages, some postcards and a brochure. His hands trembled when he held them out to me, and I saw his eyes were shining.

"The *Camino del Norte!*", he told me, breathlessly. "You must choose the *Camino del Norte*. I followed it, yes . . . but only the second time. Because, you see, I was not allowed to take it."

"Not allowed?"

"In a manner of speaking. When I came to get my *credencial* like you, here, today, I encountered a man who . . ."

I could see a spark of hatred in his eyes.

". . . who told me I was too old," he spat. "That I wouldn't make it. It is because of him that I first took the *Camino Francés*. But I was angry, sir, angry! And the next year I told my wife: this time I am taking the *Norte*. And I did."

"And what happened?"

29

"What happened was, of course, that I didn't have the slightest problem. I averaged thirty kilometres a day! And I am no athlete."

There was a silence. I was a bit embarrassed by such an emotional outburst. That was because I did not yet know the Way.

I suddenly jumped. The man had grabbed my arm.

"Do it, monsieur!" he shouted. "Take the North Way. It's the most beautiful, believe me, the most beautiful."

I thanked him and fled, telling myself that this pilgrimage was clearly just for the lunatic fringe and I had best stick to my earlier idea of a simple hike in the mountains. I decided I would definitely take the High Route across the Pyrenees.

Eight days later, I set off for Santiago de Compostela, along the *Camino del Norte*.

5

Setting Off

I took the TGV to Hendaye. To be honest, I felt rather ridiculous travelling in a comfortable carriage at 200 k.p.h. kitted out like a pilgrim. And when we had arrived, and I stood alone on the platform, I began to realise just how anachronistic this all was. In the twenty-first century, what was the point of following such a path *on foot*? There was no obvious answer. But there was no time to explore this question more deeply; a cold wind was sweeping across the empty platform, as the Atlantic squalls quickly dispelled the May warmth. The other passengers had already gone, happily pulling their little wheelie suitcases behind them. I straightened out my badly fastened pack and hoisted it on my back. It already seemed heavier than it did at home.

On that first night in Hendaye I limited my efforts to crossing the square in front of the station and walking up a charming, and thus touristy, little street to the hotel where I had booked a room.

I had decided to grant myself this luxury for the last night before my departure: a real room in a proper hotel, with a capital H on a blue plaque and a single star (let's not be extravagant). When you are about to leave France to go wandering like a vagabond, there is no good reason to deny yourself the pleasure of having, one last time, a cramped room that smells of damp, a shower suitable for a toddler, an unpleasant proprietor who looks at you disapprovingly and demands you pay in advance, and drunks yelling under your window until the early hours of the morning. It is good to take with you a fresh memory of the country you are leaving. Reinvigorated by this experience and not having slept a wink all night, I found myself outside at 7.30 a.m. Without losing time by exploring Hendaye (no doubt a delightful town), I headed for the Santiago Bridge, a motorway flyover which spans the River Bidassoa and leads to Spain.

I had memorised very precise descriptions from the guidebook I had brought and already read a hundred times. Every crossroads was familiar. Even the main roads had a certain charm for they lent colour – tarmac grey – to the lines on the map. During those first moments of walking, you have no idea yet what lies ahead, how vast the Way is, how enormous. Walking through Irún I simply felt I was going on a long stroll – and that I had picked the wrong place for it.

Then I had suddenly left the town behind and I was still walking. I bought a bottle of water from a grumpy grocer. As I left the shop I realised that it was located just before the junction that takes the Way into the countryside. All the pilgrims must stop there, and their appearance was no longer a distraction but a routine, and not an especially pleasant one given their consumer habits. After much deliberation I had decided to buy only a half-bottle, for there would surely be places to find water along the way. The man took my thirty-five cents with a deep sigh.

My thirst quenched, I crossed the main road and took the path which led at last into a verdant landscape. A little further on, crossing a stone bridge over a little brook, it really started to look like something from antiquity. My novice pilgrim emotions were powerfully stirred. I wanted to sing. I felt I would soon be wandering through the legendary forest of Brocéliande, where I would encounter knights in armour and find ancient monasteries. As you may have already noticed, I get easily carried away. The only way I have found of reining in my wild imagination is to make up stories and write novels. But now, without knowing it, I had found a new cure for over-excitement by setting off for Santiago. The Camino is full of contrasts and will never fail to bring flights of fantasy firmly back to earth. It always, if I can put it like this, keeps the pilgrim in line. In fact, the magical countryside I thought I had plunged into was nothing but a false alarm, just an appetiser. Very soon the cinderblock walls were back, along with the miserable vegetable patches, outdoor toilets, and schizophrenic dogs, shackled in chains but trained to transform into baying hounds of hell whenever a passer-by approaches.

Elation vanished immediately. Maybe there are artificial ways to stimulate it. But you would need a lot of alcohol or cannabis to believe these mongrels were fire-spitting demons, or the old lady swearing at them from her doorstep was Don Quixote's Dulcinea.

The truth is that disenchantment with the world is considerably speeded up on the Camino, even though it is supposed to revive emotions from the depths of time. I would say it takes about two hours to come back to reality and see it with open eyes: the Camino is a path, and that's it. It goes up, it goes down, it gets slippery, it makes you thirsty, it is well or badly marked, it goes along roads or loses itself in woods, and each of these circumstances offers advantages – but also a fair few inconveniences. In short, once you leave the realm of dream and fantasy, the Way abruptly appears as what it is: a long ribbon of effort, a slice of the ordinary world, a test for body and mind. You will have to struggle hard to give back a bit of magic to it.

In any case, the walker's attention is very soon monopolised by a more prosaic concern: not getting lost. To avoid going astray you must always keep a lookout for the signs that indicate the route. There are several types of Camino waymarks, and the pilgrim quickly learns to spot them. Finding them becomes second nature. In a vast landscape, full of details, of foregrounds and backgrounds, the pilgrim's eye, like radar, instantly detects the marker stone, the arrow, the sign that points towards Santiago. These signs are scattered here and there with no discernible regular intervals between them. Over the centuries they have gradually been put at those places where they are necessary. Here, a crossroads where those who pass may hesitate: a marker stone will clearly indicate the right choice. There, a straight section of path that seems to have gone on too long without a marker; maybe you should retrace your steps? And then a reassuring yellow arrow encourages you to continue. These big yellow arrows, easy and cheap to make, are the foot-soldiers of signage, while the stones, with their ceramic scallop shells are more like the officers. Although they have been in the same spots since the Middle Ages, these waymarks have since been modernised: a blue background in the same shade as the EU flag, a stylised shell with a fan of lines coming together in a point. Sometimes on the edge of a town or near a major road junction, you will find the same shell spread across a huge sign, accompanied by intimidating inscriptions such as "Beware, pilgrims crossing!", The walker is thus assured that he is on the right track, and that he may well get run over.

But on this first morning I was still a beginner. A novice reader, unaccustomed to deciphering the Saint-James script, I had to keep scanning the path for yellow lines or blue scallop shells. Once I got out of Irún, the arrows led me to Mount Jaizkibel, which the Way ascends before going along the summit.

It is a pleasant little mountain, offering a panorama right across the valley below. From time to time, a viewpoint will reveal a vast expanse of land and sea stretching off into the horizon. And you begin to understand that the wonders of the Way do indeed exist but they are not constant. You have to seek them out, some would say you have to deserve them. The pilgrim does not walk along with an ecstatic smile fixed on his lips like an Indian sadhu. He winces and whines and curses and complains, and it is against this backdrop of constant little woes that every now and then something pleasant turns up, appreciated all the more for being unexpected, a splendid view, an emotional moment, a fraternal encounter. This first stage is one of the most beautiful on the *Camino del Norte*. After the slopes of Jaizkibel, the path drops down to a small estuary between two steep banks. You have to take a ferry to get across, a tiny motorboat crammed with locals on shopping trips. From the quay, on the other side, you go right, towards the sea and then walk back up a steep hill overlooking a pretty little red and white lighthouse. The coastal path follows the shore at a great height and through the frequent gaps there are views over the sea to the horizon.

The scenery here – heathland and scrub, black cliffs and the dark blue sea with a swell rolling in from the ocean – looks more like Ireland than Spain. Spoilt by this first stage of beauty and wilderness, the pilgrim may also take false hope and imagine that the Camino will grant him similar favours all the way.

Let him dream. Very soon he'll be walking through charmless suburbs and alongside motorways. At the start of the journey, the novice needs encouragement and the landscape does its best to oblige. For, having come to the end of the steep and rocky coast that he has followed for several hours, the walker now discovers a new splendour: the bay of San Sebastián spreads out at his feet. The perfect curve of its beaches, hemmed with a ribbon of foam, the majestic seafront, designed for seeing as much as being seen, the straight grid of its long avenues with people strolling along the wide pavements – everything in Donastia (the other name for San Sebastián) is there to delight the pilgrim who has now had his fill of sombre rocks and seagulls. Then begins a long descent down well-maintained cobble paths winding through terraces planted with tamarisks.

6

A Savage in the City

It had started to rain as I was walking down, and San Sebastián was soon veiled in fine mist, which added to its charm. But unfortunately this surfeit of beauty brought a more material concern: I had to get my waterproofs out of my rucksack, put them on and discover their faults for the first time. On my first day anxiety had made me rush, and I had walked a long way without stopping to eat or drink. The sight of the city suddenly reminded me of these necessities: the desire to sit down in front of a good meal quickly made me forget the beauty of the sights. For once my stomach was bigger than my eyes.

On this subject, there was my first incident, one that I hesitate to relate. But I will report it anyway for in my opinion it marks a significant stage in adaptation to the condition of pilgrim. The walker turns into a down-and-out very quickly. However refined and civilised you may be when you set off, it won't take long for the Way to rob you of your modesty as well as your dignity. Without quite becoming an animal you are no longer entirely human. This could be the definition of the pilgrim.

Halfway down the endless descent into San Sebastián, and perhaps distracted by these digestive thoughts, I was overcome with an irrepressible desire that the constipation of the last few days easily explained. Every step echoed most painfully in my stomach. I had reached the place on the hillside where rare trees were planted among paths and ponds: it was a public park. It was still raining and there was no-one in sight. What should I do? In other circumstances I don't doubt that I would have displayed heroism and continued the descent, holding myself back. To my great surprise, the pilgrim inside me demanded action of an entirely different kind. I put my rucksack on a stone table intended for family picnics and, having stepped over a well-trimmed hedge, squatted down in a flowerbed. As I went back to my rucksack a sudden fear struck me: perhaps someone had seen me? The park was open on all sides and on this steep hill the whole slope was visible from the top. What if I were arrested, perhaps charged with relieving myself in a public park in the Basque Country? I imagined for a moment the scandal in Paris at the Institut de France on quai Conti. And with this, I burst out laughing, put on my rucksack and carried on down without looking back. I pulled my hood over my head and vanished from the scene of my crime, a grey shadow amidst the gloom of the rain-soaked trees. It is through experiences like this that you gauge your new weakness, which is a great strength. You are now nothing and nobody, just a poor pilgrim whose actions are of no account. Had I been discovered, no-one would have prosecuted me, they would have just sent me packing with a kick up the arse like the insignificant vagabond I had already become.

Maybe that is one of the motives for going on the pilgrimage. In any case, it was for me. As life weighs you down with responsibilities and experiences, it seems more and more impossible to become someone else, to cast off the heavy cloak of conformity that your commitments, successes and mistakes have fashioned for you. But the Way accomplishes that miracle.

In the years before, I had clothed myself in a succession of socially prestigious glories but I didn't want them to become the luxurious shroud of my freedom. And now the ambassador served in his residence by fifteen people in white jackets, the academician received beneath the cupola with a roll of drums, has just been running between the tree trunks of a public park to hide the most insignificant and most disgusting of crimes. Believe it or not, it was a useful experience and one that I would almost recommend to other people.

It was still drizzling as I walked across San Sebastián, with its wide, straight avenues, to the seafront. This first stage continued to teach me about my new condition: a pilgrim never arrives anywhere. Pilgrims pass through, that is all. They are immersed in the place where they are (their pedestrian status puts then in direct contact with the location and its inhabitants) and at the same time they are utterly detached from it, for their destiny is always to move on. Their haste to depart, even if they take care to go slowly, is written all over them. They are not like tourists: tourists may rush round the monuments but at least they have come there to see them. The reason for the presence of the pilgrim is to be found elsewhere, at the end of his quest, in the square outside the cathedral of Santiago de Compostela.

In the refined, upper-class San Sebastián, with its luxurious seafront, opulent villas and fine boutiques, I immediately understood how insignificant I had become, almost invisible. No-one sees the pilgrim. He does not count. His presence is ephemeral, negligible. The people in the street go about their business, and even those who are just taking a walk or doing their daily jog seem not to notice this lower form of life who is already rather dirty and badly shaved, plodding along bowed down by the weight of his crooked rucksack.

Having reached the Concha Bay, with its perfect crescent, I walked down onto the sand. The rain had driven away walkers from the shoreline, and the beach was deserted. But then there was a comforting burst of sunshine. The horizon took on tones of emerald and indigo, contrasting with the green of the islands in the bay and the coastline. I put my rucksack down, took my shoes off and went to bathe my feet in the warm sea. Then I came back and lay on the sand. My bare feet, red from walking, framed the perfect picture of the skyline over the sea. People had returned to the beach and their dogs were shaking themselves dry again. Neither humans nor animals paid any attention to the *Jacquet* washed up on the beach, most unsuitably dressed for such a chic holiday resort. But, like rubbish that no-one bothers to pick up because they know the sea will carry it away, the pilgrim, however out of place he is, doesn't bother the locals, who know he will be gone before long. And I soon was, especially since it had started to rain again. I walked the long beaches, went through some tunnels and soon found myself on the other side of the city at the foot of Mount Igueldo. I followed the path, which wound through some very upmarket housing developments, all with their blinds down, as one would expect out of season, and slowly but surely I left the city behind.

Though San Sebastián had several hostels for pilgrims, I had decided that from now on I would camp out.

7

First Wild Camp

This stage of the journey had been a long one, and I was panting a bit as I climbed up the slopes of Mount Igueldo. It always takes a while to get out of a city when you're on foot. On this side, San Sebastián quite quickly gives way to countryside and coastal heathland, but even so you still have to go through the last built-up areas, little villages swollen with new houses by their proximity to the city.

On a narrow path leading out of one of these suburban villages, I was pleasantly surprised to come across a friendly sign. Alongside a wall someone had set up a little table for pilgrims. Earthenware water jars were there to fill empty flasks. Protected by a little canopy there was a register where walkers could leave their comments. A notice wished them a happy pilgrimage and told them, with a precision which could have been either cruel or kind, that they had "only" another seven hundred and eighty-five kilometres to go until they reached Santiago. And, best of all, there was a stamp attached to its inkpad by a little chain so that you could authenticate reaching this stage. I hadn't managed to get a stamp on my *credencial* in San Sebastián because the tourist office was shut when I went past. As a novice pilgrim I lacked the experience of old hands who get their pilgrim passports stamped in chemists, bars, post offices or even police stations. So I had left empty-handed. And so it was that on this unnamed stretch of the route, almost in the middle of nowhere, I solemnly made the first record of my journey on paper, thanks to this little stamp in the shape of a beautiful red scallop shell. I wrote a few friendly words for the stranger who had left me this gift, with the same degree of gratitude that George Brassens expresses in his *Chanson pour L'Auvergnat*. And then I walked on.

It was now late in the afternoon. The sun had returned, and I was dripping with sweat in the humid heat. I had to get a move on to find a suitable camping spot.

I noticed quite a few, but every time I got closer I decided they were too near to farms, too visible from the road, or not flat enough. At last, as night was falling, I climbed over a barbed-wire fence and found part of a field that seemed about right. Over the hedges I could see the sea stretching off to the horizon. Big cargo ships sailed by in the distance. I put up my tent, sorted out all my camping gear and cooked my dinner on the little stove.

Night fell, and I sat staring into space for quite a while before finally lying down to sleep. In one day I had lost everything: my geographical bearings, the foolish dignity that titles and social status could provide. This wasn't just some fleeting weekend experience but a new condition, one that was going to last.

While I was certainly suffering from all the discomforts and from the thought that there were a lot more to come, I also felt happy with this new asceticism. I understood how valuable it can be to lose everything, in order to find what is essential. On that first evening, I weighed up the madness of this undertaking as well as its necessity and told myself that all things considered I had made the right choice.

*

With a very small amount of training, it is easy enough to cope with the days on a pilgrimage. The nights are something else. It all depends on how easily sleep comes to you no matter where you are and who else is around. There's no justice in this: some people can fall asleep as soon as their heads touch the pillow, so soundly that even a train roaring by wouldn't rouse them. Others, including me, are used to lying awake for hours and hours, eyes wide open, legs jittery. And when at long last they manage to drift off, it only takes a creaking door, a whispered conversation, the slightest touch, to wake them up.

Of course there are always sleeping pills. But sadly I have taken so many of them in my life that they are no longer any use to me, except to add migraine to insomnia.

In these conditions, night does not bring rest but an ordeal. On the long adventure of the Way, too many sleepless nights will weigh down the pilgrim with a heavier load than his rucksack.

All along the routes to Santiago de Compostela, special hostels have been established, called *albergues* in Spanish. They are the descendants of the ancient "pilgrim hospitals" of the Middle Ages. Their special feature is the extremely low price. For just a few euros, pilgrims get a bed, shared showers, cooking facilities and often the option of a cooked meal. All this is provided with the frugality of a youth hostel, or indeed of an emergency shelter after a natural disaster. Some of these hostels are in monasteries, other more secular ones in municipal buildings. And some are privately run. I have nothing against these places. I don't mind the lack of privacy, the body odours, or the excessively warm welcome from some of the *hospitaleros*, as the staff are called in Spanish. No, the only thing that makes me uncomfortable is a terrible certainty which grips me as soon as I cross the threshold: I will surely find a bed there and maybe even board, but I won't get any sleep. Even worse, I know that in places like this, where all kinds of very different people mingle, I will be painfully reminded of the scandal of nature which allows some to sleep while others don't get a wink. This advantage alone would be enough to make me hate the privileged ones to whom the gods have granted the ability to find sleep anywhere, but it is exacerbated by their propensity, as soon as they nod off, to start snoring and thus rule out any chance of us joining them. Those responsible for this noise pollution are not always easy to spot, so you never know which ones to avoid when you choose your bed. True, the snorer is often male, extremely corpulent, as discreet and quiet during the day as he is loud once the lights are out. But I have also encountered innocent little women, fragile and delicate, whose nasal cavities transform into horns as soon as they fall asleep, blowing with all the power of Roland at the Pass of Roncevaux. Sensing that sooner or later I would do something unforgivable to one of these snorers, I decided to avoid this dangerous situation as often as possible and took a tent with me.

My earlier experience of climbing had taught me that mountain refuges involved similar ordeals to the *albergues*, and I decided long ago to avoid them by camping. Once, that used to mean carrying a heavy load. But today there are very well-designed mountain tents that weigh barely a kilo. Add to that an outdoor sleeping bag and a camping mat and you can be well equipped with less than three kilos. Even if I had to carry ten, I would find the burden negligible if it guaranteed me peaceful nights. And in any case I like sleeping out of doors. Fresh air flows through the tent, and the sleeper, or even the insomniac, can breathe more deeply, fill his lungs with the breath of nature. You can toss and turn as much as you like, spread yourself out, sing, recite poetry, put the light on: you are not disturbing anyone apart from prowling animals, which you sometimes hear scuffling about nearby.

Wild camping is strictly forbidden in Spain, even bivouack-ing (setting up a temporary shelter between sunset and sun-rise). It is of course very hard to get anyone to obey this rule. There's nothing more enjoyable than breaking an unenforce-able law. It makes you feel that you are more reasonable than the rest of society. And, as a bonus, it is a tiny act of resistance and thus a source of fraternity. For you soon discover that the people of Spain show great understanding for campers: they do not just tolerate them, they help them.

8

Fortunes and Misfortunes of the Pilgrim Camper

The first stages of the Way, from the Spanish frontier to Bilbao, hit me like one of those octopuses that fishermen tenderise by slapping them against the stones on the quayside. Even with no snorers beside me, it took me quite a while to fall sleep on the hard ground, yet the morning heat ignored such excuses and drove me out of my sleeping bag at the crack of dawn. And I rapidly discovered that the sleeping bag I had bought for the High Level Route through the Pyrenees was far too warm for late spring in Spain.

As soon as I was up, completely befuddled by lack of sleep, I had to walk until I found a café that was open. The whole camping stove ritual was far too dispiriting in the morning, and in a region with no shortage of facilities it was silly to carry on as if I was on some deserted mountainside.

The only problem is that places suitable for wild camping are rarely anywhere near cafés. Every morning I was obliged to plod for several kilometres from wherever I had pitched my tent to a place where I could gulp down a *café con leche*; I did so in a deep coma, not something known to be compatible with walking. This was usually the moment when the Way chose to slip off into the woods, to follow charming little paths where you would love to linger in delight were it not 6 a.m. and you not ravenously hungry.

Here and there mountain streams and springs were indicated to pilgrims so they could drink and wash. Those who haven't had the opportunity to take a shower in an *albergue* should grab the chance wherever it presents itself. On some mornings I immersed myself in icy water when the Way had not deigned to put a café on my path. What in other circumstances might have been a pleasure becomes one more endurance test. When you've finally reached a village and had a coffee and snack, exhaustion, lack of sleep and the feeling that you are stewing in your dirty clothes neutralise the caffeine hit, and you spend the rest of the day with a thick head.

As it crosses Euskadi, the Camino follows the coast. Holiday resorts with unpronounceable names alternate with stretches of deserted shore. The persistent nausea of the novice hiker has made my memories of this time rather hazy. I am left with a jumble of images: tourist cafés on a chic seafront, with couples walking their dogs, carefree cyclists, and English visitors waiting with ill-disguised impatience for the first drink of the day; roads running along the shoreline and by sea walls made of rocks; luxury houses in a seaside resort called Getaria, proud to have been the birthplace of the great fashion designer Balenciaga, dazzlingly green little valleys with charming white houses nestling in them.

You should always be very wary of green areas. A lush, verdant landscape can only mean one thing: rain. My memories of the scenery in this first week may be confused, but I can recall the downpours I endured in the Basque Country with great clarity. In Deba I had to make a stop in a hotel to dry out all my kit. This was the beginning of a pattern that would last all the way to Santiago de Compostela: two or three days of camping followed by a night in a small hotel. Bound, despite myself, by the pilgrim's vow of poverty, I took comfort in the fact that a hotel room cost only about three times as much as a night in an *albergue* and so I wasn't spending more than the "normal" Jacquet.

It was on this stretch of the Way that I found the most unusual places to camp. I spent one night in a narrow cove between two cliffs, a place where layers of rock, weathered by coastal erosion, descend like the teeth of a giant comb into the tousled hair of the waves. Parallel lines of pink and grey rock spread out from the shoreline towards the horizon. When the tide is out, you can walk along this magical causeway paved with rocks, with little lines of water rippling between them. I was blessed with a glorious sunset. The last rays of the sun spread their light all the way from the horizon to where I stood, following the straight tracks marked out by the rocks just above the surface of the sea. The sky was the purest blue. I had almost regained normal consciousness, restored by a hotel meal the night before. My tent was carefully erected by the edge of the cliffs, in a field. The farm labourers had left the field as evening fell, carrying on their shoulders the long rakes they use for gathering up the hay. The night looked peaceful, and with a bit of luck I would get some sleep. Alas, an hour later a storm suddenly swept in, battering the coast with incredible violence, and I spent the night hanging onto my tent to make sure it didn't get blown away. Soaked yet again, dizzy and exhausted, I got on my way at daybreak. Those rocks reaching into the sea looked grey in the rain. I calculated that it was four kilometres to the next café. . . .

9

Solitudes

Throughout the first stages of the journey, I was on my own, or almost. Very occasionally I would see another pilgrim, and I kept my distance. The fact that I didn't sleep in the *albergues* was a big disadvantage in the gregarious world of Santiago hikers. In these gathering places people are forced to meet through the various rituals like the choice of a bed ("top or bottom?"), a serious decision which usually starts off the first conversation.

On the North Route, the smaller number of pilgrims means you are unlikely to meet anybody as you walk. If you are walking quickly, it can happen that you overtake the odd group or individual. You first glimpse them from behind. A scallop shell swinging from their rucksack beats time with every step they take. You get closer, and as you go past you call out the ritual "*Bon Camino*". This is not Spanish but a kind of Esperanto used by everyone from Germans to Australians. It certainly does not mean that the person speaks Castilian, and if you launch into the language of Cervantes, the chances are that the pilgrims will shake their heads and look embarrassed.

I adapted easily to my solitude. It even seemed to be something necessary so that I could completely absorb my new identity of wandering ascetic, as required by the Way. Whenever I caught sight of couples or groups I felt that they lacked something essential for the full pilgrim experience. Just as on those language courses where you'll never learn to speak like a native if you're surrounded by your compatriots, it seemed to me that the only answer was total immersion. To become a true pilgrim I had to surrender to silence, meditation and grime, to which no familiarity or companionship opposed a limit.

Thus I had won my first stripes in the Santiago hierarchy by scrupulous solitude in the first few days. My chin was already covered with stubble, my clothes were stained with mud and whatever food I had managed to cook on my camping stove. And my brain, pounded by walking, had dissolved into a fog of nausea and fatigue. I had lost my habitual patterns of thought and was ready to undergo the great transformation that would give me the mindset of a true pilgrim.

Things that had not mattered until then, things I did not even know about before I left, were steadily becoming major issues. Spotting the signs on the path that keep you from getting lost, getting the shopping you need for meals, finding some flat ground to erect your tent before it gets too late, working out what you can carry on your back when the load is already too heavy – these matters preoccupy the *Jacquet* to the point where he is enslaved by them day and night.

Once the transformation happens, you are a stranger to the person you were before, and then you are ready to meet new people.

The conclusion of this initial acclimatisation period corresponded more or less with my arrival at the monastery of Zenarruza. I approached the monastery along an ancient, paved track that plunged me straight into the Middle Ages. This tree-shaded, sunken *calzada* was still muddy from the rain of the night before, but once I got to the end I was welcomed by bright sunshine sparkling on the hedgerows and lending a luminous glow to the soft green meadows on the surrounding hillsides. From the hilltop monastery there was a stunning view over the Basque countryside, beneath a deep blue sky with big white cotton-wool clouds. In front of the monastery church, the final stage of a Way of the Cross was marked by three granite columns. An archway led into a courtyard bordered by the church on the right and the monastic buildings on the left. There was no sign of life anywhere. The other end of the courtyard opened onto a park whose lawns stretched up towards the woods. There was a little shop selling things made by the monks; it was closed but it had an intercom buzzer to call the brother in charge. I pressed the button. A crackly voice asked me to go and have a look at the new building and wait outside the kitchen. I then noticed that behind the church and facing the panorama of the hills there was indeed a small building, very recently built, with floor-to-ceiling windows, which looked residential. Turning the corner I arrived on the terrace which stretched out in front of it. I waited.

Following the instinct of the pilgrim I had become, I put my rucksack down and massaged my shoulders, then stretched out on the ground, resting my head against the wall, my face turned to catch the last of the setting sun. Once you start to let yourself go, it's a slippery slope. So I soon took off my shoes, then my socks, and began a close inspection of my toes. It was at that moment that a strange-looking little man in overalls appeared in front of me. Balding head, keen eyes, a little smile on his lips, Brother Gregorio welcomed me. With an air of authority, he showed me the pilgrim dormitory as I followed him around in my bare feet – a tiny room on the side of the modern building, which you enter through a discreetly concealed door. The furniture consisted of metal bunks and a formica-topped table; it could accommodate eight people. The brother delivered his standard pilgrim introduction without paying me any attention. When he had finally finished, I got the chance to ask if I might be allowed to put up my tent outside. The garden where I had seen the three calvary crosses was particularly appealing. Sheltered by a tall plane tree, the little green triangle offered a very nice view of the hills and also had a public bench. Gregorio said there was no problem for me to set up camp there.

At that very moment, a group of four women appeared, out of breath from coming up the slope. Catching sight of them, Gregorio's face lit up.

With me he had been somewhat mechanically polite; with the newcomers he displayed a great deal more enthusiasm. Having learned they were Australians he starting babbling away in English. With great excitement, he took them one after another by the arms and showed them the dormitory. I heard him giving his spiel again but this time with a lot more chuckles. The women laughed in turn and he responded with louder chuckles. When he came out, three Austrian women turned up, which seemed to make him even more excited. He spoke German with as much pride as he attempted English.

He waited outside with me while the women were settling in. They all came back out and sat on the ground as I had done, but Gregorio remained standing. He told us he had originally been a monk in this monastery but had then quit Holy Orders for some twenty years. He had travelled all over the world, he went on, though without making it at all clear what he had actually done in all that time. While sharing all this with us, he kneaded the shoulder of a huge Austrian woman. When she had arrived she had thrown off her enormous rucksack which she handled as easily as if it were a small cushion, and given me a look so greedy it made me rather nervous.

But the monk had now released the Austrian and was massaging the shoulder of one of the Australians. Pale and tight-lipped, she seemed a lot less voracious than her Teutonic companion. But Gregorio was so funny – and after all he was a monk – that the serious pilgrim put up with it. Indeed, she seemed to find it rather pleasant.

Gregorio spoke of the ships on which he had embarked to cross distant seas. He told us entertaining tales about Japan and the Japanese, Argentina and the Argentinians, America and the Americans. As he described each new step on his travels, he would proudly use words he had learned from a wide range of languages, punctuating his delivery with bursts of laughter. Finally, he said, after twenty years of wandering, he had decided to return to Ziortza and to his monastery in Zenaruzza. They seemed to have no problem welcoming him back, especially because his linguistic talents made him very suitable for the job of *hospitalero*.

He arranged to meet us for Vespers, if we wanted to come. And after that he would serve us dinner. Once Gregorio had gone, the dance of the showers began. I had a certain advantage being the only man since the bathrooms were separated into men's and women's. After that I went off to set up my tent and sort out my bedding.

When I got back, all the women had disappeared and I assumed they had gone to the church. A shrill bell summoned us to evening prayer.

Vespers in Zenarruza

I took a walk around the monastery buildings and went into the church, a massive, sombre Romanesque building. The eighteenth-century high altar was made of gilded wood, backed by an ornate altarpiece with sculptures and twisted columns, rising up almost into the vault of the choir. It was hard to see it properly in the darkness. But suddenly an invisible hand flicked a switch, and the altar lit up. The gleaming gold, the flesh tones of the statues and the flashes of blue in the panels of the altarpiece shone out against the bleak background of bare stone. Soon the monks in their scapulars entered in single file and sat down, forming a half circle. There were six of them, including Gregorio. He was unrecognisable. The puckish, ribald joker was now a solemn, grave-faced monk, gazing in anguish at the crucified Christ.

My fellow pilgrims, the Austrians and Australians, had spread themselves around on the wooden pews. Their different postures gave some idea of their spiritual leanings. One was staring up in the air, eyes fixed on the stone vault, and it looked like all she was seeking in the silence of the church was to attain Oneness. Another, on her knees and busily crossing herself, indicated her belief in Christ. And a third, surely a Lutheran, leafed through one of the psalters that a monk had distributed at the start of the service, no doubt unable to imagine prayer without the help of a scripture. Unfortunately the psalters were in Spanish, so that she faced not only the obscurity of the psalms but also impenetrable Castilian. In a row near mine I spotted the sturdy Austrian who responded to my glance with a broad smile. Without wishing to delude myself about how I looked, I had the strong impression that it was the male in me that was having this effect. This one didn't seem to be waiting for the resurrection of the flesh in the afterlife; she looked like she firmly intended to make the most of it in this one.

The monks had begun chanting. One was playing a harmonium. The power and solemnity of Spanish mysticism was written on their faces, which were etched by privation. Three of them had black beards making them look like figures from an El Greco painting.

The intoxicating magic of prayer had gripped us all. One of the things that is so special about the Way is that it can offer pilgrims – whatever their reasons for making the pilgrimage – moments of unexpected religious intensity. The more banal the pilgrim's daily life becomes, dominated by painful blisters or rucksacks that are too heavy, the more powerful these flashes of spirituality. At first the Way demands that we forget our souls and submit to our bodies, to their pains and countless needs. And then, breaking into this tedious routine, which has turned us into two-legged beasts of burden, there comes one of those moments of pure ecstasy, in a simple chant, a meeting, a prayer, and the body breaks open, shatters into pieces and releases a soul that you thought had been lost.

I was immersed in such reflections when the church door was suddenly thrown open. The monks didn't blink and carried on chanting. But for us pilgrims, whose faith was weak and whose ecstasy fragile, this intrusion broke the flow of spiritual energy. Someone came in, then it was two people, four, and more and more until there were about twenty of them. They were Spanish, men and women, and they all looked like they were past retirement age. They were dressed in white T-shirts and trousers, and most of them had cameras. Flashes went off in the darkness. The intruders were calling out to each other in what they assumed were low voices but which were enough to drown out the gentle sounds of Gregorian chants. Completely unabashed, the visitors wandered around, crossing themselves and clumsily genuflecting until they finally sat down on the pews. The disturbance continued as they noisily flicked through the pages of their psalters. The more experienced ones helped the others find the right psalm numbers then tried to join in the antiphon, chanting out of tune. As if in response to some mysterious signal, after five minutes of these shenanigans the visitors all rose and left together, not neglecting to take a few more photos on their way out and to open the creaky door dozens of times.

Vespers came to an end in an atmosphere ruined by the interruption. When we all met outside the church porch, the louts who had burst in were the main topic of conversation. The general theory was that they must have been a coach party, and the picturesque monastery was a stop on their itinerary. After their flying visit they had got back on board and must already be on their way to the next attraction.

So when we went back to pick up our rucksacks, we were rather surprised to find these supposed tourists still there. Not only that, but they were pulling their wheelie suitcases down the paths of the park in the direction of the new building, which on one side housed the tiny pilgrim dormitory. As we went round the building we saw them heading for the main entrance, which had grand glass doors and a marble floor.

A little later on Gregorio came back and we asked him what was going on. He explained that they were a group on a course. They were renting guest rooms in the monastery – the ones for which this comfortable new building had been constructed. The respectful tone in which he spoke of these visitors suggested that their stay must have been quite lucrative for the monastery.

"What are they doing here?"

"They are on a retreat."

"What kind of retreat?"

"They're doing yoga."

We then remembered that the words "Yoga Group" were printed on the back of their white T-shirts. And two of our group who had followed them into the park to take photos reported that several of our new neighbours were sitting in the lotus position outside the monastery and appeared to be bidding farewell to the setting sun.

It is with experiences like this that the pilgrim measures the changes in this world. If the pilgrimage to Santiago de Compostela seems to be enjoying a new lease of life, it is no longer the great path of the faithful that it once was. Today the Camino is just another one of the products on offer to consumers in the grand bazaar of postmodernity. Practically minded, the monks, noticing this new diversity, have adapted their services to suit individual needs. They were quick to evaluate the resources of the various groups who might seek their company. To tourists they offer monastery products (postcards, cheese, jams) at high prices. For the "Yoga Group", they have luxury rooms in the new building. As for the impoverished pilgrims, they got the measure of them long ago. Those who knock on their door are the poorest or most tight-fisted, because a fairly comfortable room in a private hostel less than a kilometre away could be had for 16 euros . . . Tradition demands that the monks provide for them, but only the bare minimum.

Confirmation of this came at dinnertime. While the sun-worshippers were assembled in a well-appointed dining hall, at 7.30 p.m. Gregorio brought us our pittance, hot from the kitchens. Probably made from the leftovers of the previous "Yoga Group", the dish wasn't bad. But its presentation in a great big square mess tin and the fact that Gregorio put this on the floor made it hard to avoid the impression that our dinner was a bowl of dog food.

But we were too hungry to care. All eight of us sat on the ground on the terrace, eating and chatting merrily. At the request of my sister pilgrims, I demonstrated my little camping stove and made *tisanes* for everyone. Hung on a length of string using the clothes pegs that none of us had forgotten to bring, our socks flapped in the wind like pennants over the camp of some army in the field.

The yoga people re-emerged, fully fed and warmed by wine. A little flurry of interest in our group ran through the retreating retirees. The word "Compostela" circulated from mouth to mouth. Finally, some of the boldest approached, cameras in hand. They were not going to go so far as to address us. In any case, the sounds we made as we chewed our monk mash probably made them wonder whether we had the gift of speech. But at least we offered a picturesque tableau, worthy of a place in their holiday album. Cameras clicked. We adopted very relaxed poses during the photo session, playing exactly the role of savages that we were allotted – a role which I must admit required very little effort at that moment.

After that, the two groups ignored each other. As the sun went down, it was time to unwind, and we leaned back blissfully against the warm stone walls. We talked about the Camino, starting with the inevitable question: "Where did you set off?" The exchange of sticking plasters and blister pads deepened our communion. I tried to make the Austrian woman – who was still pursuing me assiduously – understand that the Way had worn me out. No doubt accustomed to such disappointments, she rolled an enormous joint and took her revenge by not offering me a puff.

I went to lie down in my tent, at the foot of my Way of the Cross. And to round off all the muddle within these medieval walls now dedicated to sun-worshippers, I watched a US TV series on my iPad. Just before I fell asleep, a noise outside made me fear that the Austrian was about to slip into my tent, taking advantage of the dark to launch a final offensive and take possession of me. But it must have been the wind or an animal. Silence returned. And, since human nature is contradictory, I felt a moment's regret . . .

As I said farewell to the monastery of Zenarruza the next morning, I felt transformed. This stopover marked the end of a first week of acclimatisation and voluntary solitude. Now I had moved on to the level of sociable pilgrim.

But still I hadn't reached the stage where I wanted to set off as part of a group. Besides, everyone keeps his own company on the Camino. Pilgrims meet up in the evenings in the towns on the way and in the hostels. But apart from groups formed from the very start, like our Australian friends, they walk alone during the day, or, if they do join up it is just a temporary association. So, for example, when I met the Austrians again further on, I noticed that the trio had broken up.

Yet though I walked alone I no longer needed solitude as I had in the first days. I felt sufficiently adapted to the Way, sufficiently part of my new pilgrim self, to be able to welcome new encounters and fraternise with my fellow pilgrims, who were all so different.

11

Marathon and Santiago, One Struggle!

The physical problems brought on in the first few days by my new status as pilgrim were still there but had become much more specific: dreadful pain on the soles of my feet, just behind the toes. It was quite unbearable, but still it seemed like some kind of progress. I was convinced that all my discomfort – sleepless nights, aches and pains, hunger, thirst – had shifted down into my legs, and then concentrated under my feet.

Pilgrim's feet! A pathetic concern, but a major one on the Camino. At every stop on the journey, you have to lavish care on these extremities the importance of which one does not appreciate enough in everyday life. Some pilgrims go through a living nightmare with their feet – one that they are very keen to share with others. Rare are those who suffer in silence. Unlike other, more intimate parts of the body which modesty precludes exposing, feet are willingly displayed in public. They are thrust under the noses of the healthy, to elicit their opinions and in the hope, perhaps, that their sympathetic gaze on the blisters, abrasions, Achilles tendinitis, and so on will have a healing effect. Shops near the Camino and chemists above all are jammed with people who are itching to remove their shoes and expose their injured feet. In a chemist shop in the Basque Country I witnessed an elderly Italian, a very dignified man who no doubt had an important position in a business or university, insisting on lifting up his leg to put a bleeding foot on the counter, a malodorous battlefield of a foot, with the mud-stained remnants of plasters stuck uselessly over its craters. The poor pharmacists were shouting at him in Spanish to desist. Their faces expressed their deep despair at having the misfortune to be placed by destiny in the dreaded vicinity of the Camino. Selling an antibacterial lotion to a walker who has had the decency to explain his problem without taking his shoes off was just about acceptable. But people like this one, who, incapable of expressing themselves in Castilian, resort to the form of physical Esperanto that consists of brandishing their sanies in full view of other customers, clearly filled them with a disgust they could no longer conceal. Their only response was to repeat certain numbers, louder and louder. The uncomprehending Italian pushed his foot further forwards on the counter, knocking over perfume testers and plant-based anti-obesity products. In the end I had to translate what turned out to be the timetable of the bus that went to the nearest hospital.

Once the pilgrim has managed to overcome these inconveniences and attained the blessed state of calluses on the soles of his feet, he safeguards his achievements every evening by taking care to remove his shoes as soon as he reaches the place where he will spend the night. *Jacquets* taking their after-dinner strolls are immaculately shod in flip-flops, Crocs, or sandals. Indeed, that is how they recognise each other. But I wasn't there yet and my blisters still caused me great pain. Through my mountaineering experience, I had fallen into the sin of pride. I had never had a blister when climbing and deduced from this that I risked nothing on my path to Santiago de Compostela. I was completely wrong. The shoes I wore in the mountains, "approach shoes", are usually made of soft leather with synthetic lining and are intended to be used on slopes (ascent or descent). And as their name suggests, they are only worn for relatively short walks during the approach, at a slow pace. The Camino is something else: hours and hours of fast walking on flat ground. It is hot. Every morning you set off again on the same Calvary lasting eight or ten hours, walking on sore lesions that have hardly eased. If, like me, you have been stupid enough to buy shoes just before starting and have not broken them in yet, the result is catastrophic. The ones I had chosen were too small, and uncomfortable. I had shown myself to be careless, presumptuous, and stingy. Russians (as my son always reminds me) say that misers always pay twice. That certainly applied to me, and I had to buy other shoes en route. It was in Guernica that I made the switch. It seemed to me that a martyred city should be able to understand and ease my suffering. The new shoes were certainly a better fit (I still have them on my feet this morning as I am writing this). But if they were the basis for my future peace of mind, they still did not have the immediate power to repair the damage done by their predecessors (which I had surreptitiously dumped in a large bin in Guernica's famous covered market). I had to suffer in silence and endure the pain that went through my body at every step. Still, I had faith: as I walked on, the pain would flow down into the ground through the soles of my new shoes. In the Middle Ages people believed that if they slept with their bare feet resting on a dog's back, their rheumatism would be discharged into the body of the animal. I was starting to think this might be true. As I limped on, wincing at every step, I did so in the hope that the Camino would soon absorb the last stigmata of my suffering.

This was my state of mind as I arrived in Bilbao on a beautifully sunny Sunday morning. Approaching cities on foot is always tiresome and complicated. Later on I would manage to struggle through city outskirts without cheating. But I have to admit that on the outskirts of Bilbao, with blood on the soles of my feet, I gave in. Seeing a bus going in the right direction, I took a seat for the last few kilometres through the maze of factories and warehouses that surround Bilbao. The bus was empty but at the next stop two French women got on, pilgrims like me. Two middle-aged sisters in great shape and high spirits, bedecked with scallop shells. They told me this was their fourth pilgrimage. Each time they had set off from a different place. They had even done the famous Via de la Plata, the Silver Way, which starts in Seville and crosses Extremadura. What was unusual was that they had never walked all the way; they still had not reached Santiago de Compostela. Their husbands didn't seem to mind being on their own for a fortnight. But after that, either because the two women feared the men would not be there any more if they stayed away longer, or because they were pining for their affection, they always preferred to go home. Their terminus, this time, would be Santander.

Braver than me, they got off the bus at a stop which would let them go down into Bilbao from above by first ascending Mount Avril. I would have rather been seen as a cheat than risk opening the scabs on my feet, and I said goodbye to the two sisters, staying comfortably in my seat. Only a bit further on, when they had vanished from sight, did I notice the little guide-book that had fallen out of their rucksack. It was a detailed and annotated booklet which had accompanied them all the way and also described their next stops. I flicked through the pages, feeling sad. Every pilgrim carries something like this, and it reveals their temperament. Some, like me, erase the past straight away. Every day I tear out the page in my guide that describes the section of the route that I have just covered. For those who practise systematic forgetting like this, the journey is perpetually skewed; they always focus on the next day and flee the past. I did not take any notes at all on my journey and even got irritated when I saw some pilgrims at stops on the way scribbling away in their notebooks instead of enjoying precious moments of meditation. It seems to me that the past should be left to the discretion of a capricious but fascinating faculty specially made for it, known as memory. It classifies, preserves or rejects events, according to the degree of importance it attributes to them. These choices have little in common with judgements on the spur of the moment. So it is that scenes that seemed extraordinary or precious to you vanish without trace, while humble moments that you lived through without thinking about them survive and return one day because they are freighted with emotion.

For other people, and the two sisters were among them, time past is as precious as the future. Between the two there was the present – intense, ephemeral, dense – and to keep it alive, they must fill their guidebooks with annotations. That was how they used the little book they had left behind and which they must now be sorely missing. This rare document had introduced me to a different Way, and I decided to take it with me.

The bus was supposed to go to the centre of Bilbao, but people in fluorescent yellow jackets stopped it before that: the road along the River Nervion was blocked by a marathon. I had to get off and complete my journey on foot, limping. The façades of this ultramodern district glittered in the sun; in their midst the Guggenheim Museum blossomed like a glass flower.

Once again, the ambiance was eminently postmodern. Hobbling along, dirty, with my shapeless rucksack, I was following a supposedly medieval path, surrounded by creatures in fluorescent lycra, with Nike trainers on their feet and heart rate monitors strapped around their chests, who were running like gazelles through a landscape of glass and steel. It was a fine demonstration of man's conquest of nature, appropriation of the sacred and liberation from all the plagues that our medieval ancestors sought to expiate by their pilgrimages to the holy relics in Santiago de Compostela.

The marathon stewards brusquely ushered me off the pavement that was reserved for the runners. By the time I reached the old city, I had had some time to reflect on these events. And I came to the conclusion that my enterprise was not so different, essentially, from that of these narcissistic runners in their cool tech gear. The trial I had set myself was just longer and had other rules. It implied different ethics, a different aesthetic. But I had to admit that I was closer to these twenty-first-century joggers than to the real pilgrims of the first millennium.

This sporting metaphor confirmed me in my idea that after a week on the road, Bilbao was the place to stop for a complete rest if I wanted to be fit enough to go not forty-two kilometres, like the runners on the pavement, but eight hundred, because that was the challenge in this endurance test called "pilgrimage".

12

Bilbao

One week of walking is really no more than a stroll. A long, arduous and rather unusual one maybe, but hiking for seven days can still just feel like a holiday. It is only when you go beyond that threshold that you enter an entirely new realm. Day after day, the constant exertion and growing fatigue make the Way an experience like no other. In Bilbao, where I passed the seven-day limit, I suddenly felt dizzy. The temptation to stop there and then was strong. After all, I had seen enough; I felt I had now understood what a pilgrimage was like. Prolonging it would serve no real purpose. I would just pile up the days, one after another, all exactly the same. I was assailed by tempting thoughts of all the other things I could do to fill this free time. My feet still hadn't healed; they could serve as the pretext for going home early. And I could always come back another year, better prepared, to do the later stages of the Camino, and thus complete it in bits over three or four years.

To get myself a shower and a bed, I took a tiny room in a

little guest house in the heart of Bilbao. In the narrow street below, the Sunday crowds laughed and shouted until a downpour chased them all away. I dozed, still toying with the consoling thought of going home. First thing tomorrow I would find out about the trains to France. I could already see myself sitting comfortably in a carriage speeding towards the frontier. I nodded off.

But the Way is more powerful than these demons of temptation. It is skilful and sly. It allows the demons to have their say, show their hand, be convinced of their victory, and then, suddenly, it wakes the sleeper and makes him sit up in his bed, drenched in sweat. Like the statue of the Commander in *Don Juan*, the Way is there to point an accusing finger. "What? You want to give in, to face the shame of a premature return? The truth is that you are a coward. You are afraid. And you know what you're afraid of? Yourself. You are your own worst enemy. You will always find an objection to making an effort. You have no self-confidence. And I, Saint James, am offering you a unique chance to cast off your shackles, to face up to who you are and to overcome yourself."

And so you only go as far as the bathroom, you splash your face with cold water, and once again, you submit to the will of the Way.

That is how it was for me, and I suppose for many others it was similar. The most I could allow myself was a full day's rest; instead of setting off again the following morning, I would spend a day exploring the city and sleeping. Decision taken, I headed out into the streets.

The Spanish love doing the same thing together at the same time and place, which guarantees that any walk around their cities will be filled with sudden contrasts. On Sunday the Plaza Nueva, in the heart of Casco Viejo, was thick with people. Then, in an instant, it emptied and the tourists were the only ones left, like crayfish in a net. The long flight of steps up to the Basilica of Begoña was deserted until late afternoon, and Santiago Cathedral was empty until evening Mass. But at the time I visited, it was thronged with tourists, mingling with the faithful at prayer. I was exploring the choir and admiring the chapels around the apse when I spotted two pilgrims in front of me. As I have already mentioned, a pilgrim's first concern when he stops for the night is to take his shoes off. Anyone walking barefoot in a Camino city, however big, is very likely to be a pilgrim. And I had two such specimens before me. My curiosity increased when I got closer and realised they were women. When I finally overtook them and turned around, any residual doubt was dispelled: these were the two sisters from the bus. They jumped for joy when they recognised me and we left the cathedral delighted to have met again. After coincidences like this you start believing in miracles. I took them to the guest house and returned their precious guidebook. They were cooing with delight. I envied them a bit, because with my method, a happy event like this could not happen. Since I didn't keep any trace of the past on paper, there would have to be someone to tell me: "Look, I've found your memory!" But the only person who could accomplish this feat is me, and I sometimes wish someone else could do it for me.

We celebrated our fortuitous reunion on a café terrace. It already felt like we knew each other well. They told me a bit more about their lives, or rather their journeys because, as I have already mentioned, pilgrims don't usually say any more about themselves than that. I did not need to fend off their curiosity, for they only asked me about the route I was taking. They were setting off again the next morning and we would never meet again.

On my second day in Bilbao I discovered the working side of the city. At lunchtime, restaurants were packed with businessmen and executives in their suits. Bilbao's business district resembles the 8th arrondissement in Paris. I had left my rucksack at the guest house, but my flip-flops and dirty trousers were quite enough to mark me out as an extraterrestrial. Still, the good thing about cities is that everything is tolerated. The pilgrim is a foreign body but nobody notices and you can wander around like a ghost. Nonetheless, the Camino guidebooks advise staying away from the most fashionable streets where "shopkeepers do not welcome pilgrims". If a grimy hiker like me strayed into avenue Montaigne in Paris and tried to buy a pair of socks in Chanel, he would probably not be welcome either.

I refrained from any such daring activities and, after visiting the most notable churches and museums, returned to the guest house. I had not bought anything apart half a kilo of apples from a Moroccan greengrocer. He spoke French, and I asked him whether there were many North Africans in Bilbao. He answered with disgust: "We've got them all here." I left him before he could start grumbling about illegal immigrants . . .

Alone in my room, feeling more and more relaxed and refreshed, I studied my itinerary for the next day. To be honest, this was the only thing that still worried me about leaving Bilbao.

The short section of the route to Portugalete looked like it might be very depressing. According to the guidebook, it was "impossible to avoid abandoned docks, industrial wasteland, former social housing turned into squats". But to make sure that the hiker would not lose faith during these fourteen kilometres, the book added: "The pilgrim may feel out of place or lost in such a landscape but has nothing to fear. This is not the Bronx." Such a prospect was hardly ideal for getting me back on the road after the pressure-drop of a long and comfortable break.

To make matters worse, just as I was leaving the next morning it started to rain. This time it wasn't a downpour but cold, steady, penetrating rain. I took my time with settling up at reception, in no hurry to be outside. It was then that the concierge said something that came like a lifebuoy to a drowning man. "Are you going to Portugalete?" he asked me, gloomily.

The absurd comings and goings of pilgrims are of little interest to the inhabitants of the towns and cities they pass through. So it was polite of this man to ask me the question, perhaps because we were the only people who were awake in this shabby hotel, where he hadn't even switched on the lights yet. I told him yes, without much enthusiasm, and asked him the way, to prolong our conversation. "Take the first turning on the right. Then go down the steps. Make sure you go to the right platform."

"Platform?"

"We've got two métro lines here."

The métro! I had thought of everything except the existence of a métro in this city. It felt like fortune had built it just for me, and, as I was beginning to get all the right reflexes to go with my new condition, I saw the kind, protecting hand of Saint James in Bilbao's infrastructure.

Of course genuine pilgrims disapprove strongly of all such dishonest means of transport (bus, taxi, train, plane). The true *Jacquet* knows only walking and scorns the rest. I had already contravened this rule by taking a bus but had the excuse of my bleeding toes. This time I was well rested and nothing permitted me to succumb to modernity's siren songs. Had someone mentioned a train I would have rejected such an opportunity. But this was the métro. I've lived in Paris for a long time, and the métro is part of my everyday life. It is the way you get around town. Going on the underground takes nothing away from the Camino itself but merely changes the departure point within the city. This argument might appear specious and undoubtedly it is. Yet the pilgrim does not think like an ordinary mortal. He has his own joys and his own sufferings. The tribulations he inflicts on himself are of a different scale to those any more sedentary person would tolerate; in the same way his joys, or, to use a legal vocabulary, the commuting of his sentence, are regulated by a very personal penal code. In the case of the underground, judgement was handed down by the tribunal that all pilgrims have within them: I was permitted to enjoy the use of this convenience. Throughout my whole journey along the Camino, I would only have a right to two humanitarian measures: the bus to get into Bilbao and the métro to get out. And I have not regretted it.

So at the time when the Basques were going to work, I was standing on the platform of a shiny new métro. I realised how far I had adapted to my new condition as wanderer. Before, I would have felt conspicuous amidst all these neatly dressed, sleepy employees, with my rucksack and the boots I had bought in Guernica. But now it was quite the contrary: I felt completely at ease and I regarded them with curiosity and even a touch of pity.

It was still raining when I came out of the underground. The famous transporter bridge, the town's main attraction, which the two sisters had praised, was hidden behind a curtain of rain. So I decided to give it a miss and headed towards the famous bidegorri, the "red routes" (cycle lanes). I took shelter in the warehouse of an industrial adhesives factory to take out my waterproof overtrousers from my rucksack. I was happily surprised to find that they actually fitted and kept me comfortably dry.

There was no let-up in the torrential rain. On this last stage of my journey in the Basque Country, the downpour allowed me to be on my own with nature, empty and undisturbed. The rocky shore and the beaches, equipped to welcome picnickers and parasols, lay perfectly still, deserted, wrapped in watery veils like a sleeping beauty trying to hide her nakedness under the sheets.

At moments like these, in a blustery wind, soaked in salt spray and cold rain, the walker can find more joy than in the bright colours of a sunny day. The sense of being part of wild nature, of merging with it, of resisting it, yet knowing that, if it insists, one would let oneself be carried by the waves or swept away by the squalls, is a rare delight. Maybe not everyone experiences it, but the bad-weather pilgrim race does exist, and I have the privilege of being part of it.

Walking along the steep cliffs hanging over the sea, I was gradually approaching a frontier. I was leaving the Basque country and entering Cantabria. One of my last visions of Euskadi was a timeless scene that only the Way can create. At some point the arrows led me beside a motorway. It ran across a viaduct between two hills, and its deck was supported by huge, towering concrete columns. The path itself went down the hill and under the motorway, where I was sheltered from the rain. On the track here, two men were standing beside a horse, talking. One was a farm worker, the other dressed up like a *caballero* with wide leather trousers and a round-brimmed hat. He had dismounted and held the horse by its bridle. I could not hear what they were saying, but the tableau they formed on the green valley floor, dripping with rain, came straight from the palette of Murillo. It could have been anywhere, a long time ago, in the days when the horse was still man's machine, and when the land was cultivated by the peasant and guarded by the horseman. In other words, for the pilgrims, who reconstruct their own Middle Ages with every step they take, these men were contemporaries. At the same time, far above our heads, we could hear the lorries roaring by at high speed on the motorway, their axles thumping on the expansion joints of the vast bridge. Nothing could better illustrate the accumulation of time, the strata of modern consciousness in which the most recent layer is merely the highest so far, and leaves intact – albeit buried – the past that it claims to have left behind.

The *caballero* climbed back in his saddle. While I was hurrying down the hill, following the blue scallop shells of Saint James, I saw him heading up a dirt track towards brilliantly white houses surrounded by tall trees sparkling with rainwater. The happiness of the Camino is found in moments like this, moments that those who speed along the open highway of the present, on the road without obstacles, will never know.

13

On the Ferries of Cantabria

I should make it clear straight away that I did not like Cantabria. Or rather, I did not find unalloyed enjoyment on the long section of the Camino that goes through it (for I know that elsewhere, further inland, in particular around the famous Picos de Europa, the wild and rugged landscape is stunningly beautiful). The pilgrim route through this region seemed monotonous, depressing, badly planned: too many busy road-sides, too many factories and warehouses, too many empty housing estates with "For Sale" signs.

But we shouldn't forget that the pilgrim isn't a tourist. He has no right to insist on perfection all the time and, if the Basque Country spoiled him with its constant charms, that is no reason to believe he has the right to demand the same of every other region of Spain.

While most of my Cantabrian memories are of boredom and discomfort, I can still recall a few delightful moments. The province has some splendid towns, and the Way leads through a number of them. The first is Laredo, which the pilgrim approaches from above, after struggling through a motorway junction. Below, the red-tiled roofs of the old town huddle together in harmonious disorder, and as you walk slowly down towards them, you have time to admire the church towers, the pattern of narrow streets, the squares. And finally endless flights of steps lead down into the town itself. They end at a shopping street where passers-by see the pilgrim arriving out of nowhere, looking as intimidated as a contestant who has just come on stage in a TV game show.

This old quarter is charming, a perfectly pleasant place to while away some time. But unfortunately we are in Cantabria, the land of holiday villas, long since spoilt by the reckless greed of developers. The vast beach that spreads out around the edge of the town, which must once have been a deserted, infinitely poetic place, has become an endless seafront. Ill-assorted buildings, from villas to blocks of holiday flats with closed shutters, compete with each other in their breathtaking ugliness. Walking past the massed ranks of this concrete army is a deeply unpleasant experience. Perhaps the place livens up a little on the odd sunny weekend and during the school holidays. The promenade by the beach seems to welcome children, for there are playgrounds at various points. But when I came by it was deserted, save for a few elderly ladies walking their little dogs.

Occasional Camino signposts on the seafront preserve the memory of olden times, when pilgrims walked along the dunes and watched the seagulls soaring over the deserted shore. But my God, this beach is long! The last apartment blocks, right at the end, are even more hideous than the others. It is a relief to leave them behind and head towards the spit of sand which juts out between sea and river. There, suddenly, an unspoilt estuary opens up, which can be crossed on a ferry. There is no jetty; the boat simply turns round, broadside on, and you walk up a little gangplank. Nothing here can have changed much since the Middle Ages, except that the boat now has an engine. It is one of those rare harmonious moments which blot out all the rest and even make you like Cantabria, at least for the ten minutes it takes to cross the estuary. It was on this ferry that I met the man from Haute-Savoie who had set off from home two months earlier.

But my happiness did not last. I was soon walking along main roads again. The fact that these run through a lacustrine landscape is no consolation, quite the reverse. Already feeling sorry for the ducks and fish, the walker is constantly shaken by the roar of cars speeding by. The path beside the road is strewn with litter thrown out by drivers: tins, paper, cigarette packets. In Cantabria the pilgrim becomes aware for the first time that he himself is a piece of discarded waste. His slowness excludes him from normal life, makes him a thing of no importance that one splashes with mud, deafens with horns and if necessary runs over. It wasn't enough to have just become a vagrant, as I had in the Basque Country. I had to sink deeper and become a repugnant thing burrowing through filth. It would be an exaggeration to say that this experience is pleasant. Yet there is a certain pleasure in abnegation. To the pilgrim's very slow horizontal progress is added the no less progressive decline in his self-esteem – or rather, of the esteem that others have for him. Because it is common enough to say (but quite rare to experience yourself) that extreme humility is one of the roads to pride. The lower a pilgrim sinks, the stronger he feels, even to the point of feeling invincible. Omnipotence is never far from total renunciation. Reflecting on this leads you little by little to the true secret of the Way, even if you still need more time to discover it.

Cantabria is a pitiless mistress who drives us along the path to wisdom. But she can also give rewards. After a heavy dose of tarmac, she once more offers an estuary and ferry break. This one is the finest, for it is the one that leads to Santander.

Before arriving at the ferry dock, I had been walking behind a lone pilgrim for an hour or so. What was unusual about him was that he did not carry an ordinary rucksack like the rest of us but a medieval pilgrim's satchel. In his hand he held a heavy stick, much shorter and sturdier than the traditional pilgrim's staff that you see in old engravings. He was certainly unique.

The last few hundred metres before the quayside took me, for a change, through a maze of holiday homes, all closed up, of course. In surroundings like this, you soon start to feel odd. It is a bit like being in a Robbe-Grillet film. The fact that you are following an unknown, mysterious pilgrim makes it even stranger.

When I finally caught up with the pilgrim with the satchel and could see him up close, I was even more surprised. From his silhouette in the distance I had imagined he was one of those retro enthusiasts who kit themselves out with all the traditional Camino accessories, to the point where they appear to be in disguise. But in fact, apart from his stick and baggage, this man dressed ordinarily: jeans, 1960s-style waterproof jacket, leather shoes. He looked like he had just popped out for a packet of cigarettes.

We sat down at the prow of the ferry, with other pilgrims of the hi-tech hiker type, with GPS and the latest Gore-Tex boots. I complimented the man on his satchel, remarking with a smile that he was alone here in keeping up the old tradition that had endured for centuries until someone added shoulder straps to the pilgrim's satchel and thus invented the rucksack.

"Oh, so this is called a pilgrim's satchel?" he asked.

He looked glumly at his shoulder bag.

"To be honest, I've never thought about it. I just grabbed whatever I could find at home, and set off."

As I chatted with him, I realised he was completely sincere. Contrary to what I had supposed, there was no particular plan about his appearance. Instead this was someone – and I have never met anyone like him again – who approached the Camino with absolutely no anxiety and thus no preparation. He simply couldn't see any problem. He had left home with a couple of items and his satchel and started walking. That was that.

For all that he was well organised. As we approached the quayside in Santander where we would disembark, we started talking about accommodation. He had booked a room in a bed and breakfast. When we arrived he was the only one who knew exactly where he was going. I got the impression I was dealing with a species I had never met before: the executive pilgrim, efficient, practical, focused, competent. It made me want to ask what he was doing there. But I was now experienced enough to know this was not a question that one asked.

The only object that looked incongruous was his stick. When I looked at it closely, I realised that it was not a staff, even less a telescopic hiking pole of the kind most of us carried, but a simple fence post. It was of untreated wood, roughly shaped, with a point hacked out with an axe and sealed with tar. I was too curious not to ask him what he was doing with it.

"I was attacked by dogs and had to run for it. The only thing I could find to defend myself with was this fence post."

He had hung on to it, and he was now about to walk around a city with an implement worthy of a Cro-Magnon. And so the ancestral fear of dogs had added a cheerful little Neolithic accessory to the otherwise very twenty-first-century cool of this strange pilgrim who was carrying it.

When I was doing my research on the Way, I had read plenty of alarming dog stories. On their return some pilgrims gave frightening descriptions of their encounters with these animals. I had wondered how I would react if I faced one of the fierce hounds that those who had got away claimed to have confronted. Was I lucky or had they exaggerated? Throughout my journey I often heard dogs barking but they usually looked a lot less formidable than they sounded and most of them were locked behind fences or walls. I met a large number of scrawny mongrels, yappy little dogs and mangy old hounds. I came to think that all the dangerous dogs must have already eaten their fill of pilgrims and died of indigestion.

14

The Pipeline God

Santander is a pleasant city, even for a pilgrim. It has a human scale, with its narrow, sloping streets and ancient monuments, but it is also large enough for you to be completely anonymous. You can merge into the crowd without feeling like an intruder. In my regular routine of alternating camping with comfort, it was time again for me to stay in a real room. I found a bed and breakfast in the guidebook and rang them up. They had a vacancy, and I went straight there.

What I had taken to be a hotel was located on a big square in the lower town, not far from the port. At the street number indicated, I only found a residential building. The "hotel" was on the fourth floor. I rang the bell. An elderly woman, elegantly dressed and well coiffured, let me in. I thought I had rung the wrong bell, but no, this was the place. The owner – which was her – had chosen to rent out a few of the rooms in her vast apartment. Apart from these three or four rooms for tourists, everything was the same as it had always been, the old prints on the walls, the piano in the hallway, the lace doilies on the tables. Her living room, on the left after the entrance, was decorated, if that is the appropriate word, with an incredible clutter of display cases full of trinkets, velvet-draped armchairs and tapestry fireplace screens.

I walked through this bijou apartment, well aware of my somewhat rustic appearance. My landlady had the decency not to be offended. The additional revenue from renting out rooms came at the price of the inconvenience of having her cocoon invaded by malodorous and hirsute people. She gave the impression of knowing exactly what she was doing, of being well aware that this ordeal would always turn to her advantage. Civilisation would prove stronger than barbarism. After an hour, the pilgrim would emerge from his room washed, shaved and perfumed. As indeed I did.

I really liked Santander, its shopping streets, its tapas bars, its grocery stores full of what, to a Frenchman, seemed like exotic produce. My camera had broken and I bought a cheap little Kodak digital to replace it. I still have it, and it works perfectly, even if its famous manufacturer has since stopped producing them.

I would have happily granted myself a day off in this charming place but I had already lost time in Bilbao. The Way awaited me. I could feel it calling impatiently. If I had decided to stay another day, it would have bullied me with feelings of guilt and remorse. I now saw clearly that it laid down its own laws and resistance was useless.

When I returned to the bed and breakfast, my landlady was taking tea with friends in the living room. They were charitable enough to pay no heed to the zombie who glided across the Persian carpets in the hall and retired to the cubbyhole accorded him for the night. Early in the morning I left the money for the room on the piano, along with the key. And set off down the streets, which the municipal cleaners were washing down with copious quantities of water.

I have made no secret of it. I found my journey across Cantabria extremely tedious.

Trying to recall details of this leg of the Camino is equally boring. In any case, I've forgotten most of them. My memory, always a good judge, quickly deleted these stretches of monotonous coast. All that remain are a few sparse, vague recollections, which are hard to place precisely.

But I do remember quite clearly my departure from Santander, because of a sanctuary called *Virgen del mar*. I kept asking people I met for directions to this Virgin of the Sea, while I walked through endless, unprepossessing suburbs.

The Marian sanctuary I sought was some way off, and judging by the suspicious looks I got from people I asked, this ancient place of devotion was also far removed from the daily concerns of local inhabitants. Those who still knew how to find the *Virgen del mar* suggested I get a bus. To justify my insistence on walking there, I explained that nothing seemed far to me, since I still had 600 kilometres to go. Surprise quickly turned to mistrust, or even disgust, as if I were a dangerous mental patient on the loose. In some places, including these Santander suburbs, the pilgrim with his medieval reference points is like one of those knights in comedy films who have been transported into the present and wander through the traffic in their chain mail.

Apart from the *Virgen del mar*, my time in Cantabria is a complete blur. At most, a few disordered episodes float to the surface. To be honest, all the beads strung out on the long rosary of the Cantabrian coast seem interchangeable to me. I recall certain things but my capricious memory often gets the order wrong.

When I think back about this part of the Way, the first images that come to mind are always of road verges. The Basque country takes the pilgrim through trees and heaths and meadows. Cantabria subjects him to a deluge of motorways, junctions, railway tracks. I am probably very unfair, and if I take account of all the kilometres travelled, it may well be that my impression is false. But nonetheless, for me Cantabria is tarmac territory.

Without routes designed to suit them, pedestrians become the subhumans of the highway. Modern roads are built for the engine and the tyre; the leg and the shoe are unwelcome. Pilgrims following main roads can get the impression that the Camino route is not historically accurate. But exactly the opposite is true, as the guidebook never fails to remind us.

The Cantabrian section of the Camino sticks precisely to the medieval pilgrim route. The problem is that today this route is covered with roads. The path we follow is both authentic and unrecognisable. It leaves no room for dreams; indeed in some places it offers nightmares. Near Mogro, the Way follows vast metal pipes leading towards a chemical plant. For several kilometres, the pilgrim is accompanied by straight lines of pipes, in an apocalyptic setting. Camino signs are painted on the pipes every three hundred metres, not so much to indicate the way to go – there is only one – but to reassure the walker that he isn't hallucinating.

And should you weary of looking out for the sacrosanct yellow arrows, every now and then prophecies in white paint will make you pay attention again. "Jesus Saves" is written in large letters on the tiles. The invocation of Christ in this place is more likely to crush any remaining hope in the pilgrim; the only way Christ could save him would be to take him far away from these dismal pipes which stretch away to the horizon.

To complete the walker's demoralisation, the pipes run past another Cantabrian speciality: empty housing developments. During Spain's feverish construction boom, hundreds of thousands of new homes were built, which has especially affected this coastal region. The three-bedroom house or maisonette with garage is available here in a hundred variants. New housing estates are everywhere, each based on a different interpretation of the semi-detached or the terrace. Many of these creations are quite impressive and demonstrate the talents of Spanish architects. But sadly, scattered conglomerations of little family dwellings do not amount to anything like real urban planning. Thrown up in the middle of the countryside or on the edge of old villages, these estates are completely out of place. I have seen hills crowned for centuries by pretty little villages, which are now flanked by modern developments far bigger than the ancient settlement they surround. Even so, this construction boom might still be quite encouraging if people actually lived here. Unfortunately, the vast majority of the residential units are empty. Everything was planned, except who would move in. "For Sale" signs decorate the balconies. The shutters are closed. Here and there, an inhabited house, with toys on the lawn and washing hanging out of the window, only emphasises the desert around it.

When the pilgrim has finally reached the end of the pipeline, he arrives at a chemicals factory. It almost feels comforting: at least there are some human beings again. Lorries roll by. Chimneys billow out stinging smoke which is probably toxic. It isn't very nice; you might have dreamt of something a little better. But anything seems preferable to the desolation of places prepared for the living and inhabited by the silence of death.

15

Beauty Defiled

Some of my readers who have visited the Cantabrian coast as tourists will probably be incensed by all my negative comments. "What about Santillana del Mar! Comillas! Colombras!" they'll complain, places rich in history, little towns and villages rightly considered architectural gems.

These places are beautiful, I agree. But from the perspective of this narrative, a walker's perspective, they do nothing to compensate for the monotony of industrial landscapes. No doubt I visited them at the wrong time. In the depths of winter, veiled by clouds, they certainly exude a timeless poetry. Alas, under the hot June sun, these historic sites are swamped by hordes of tourists. Coaches park on their fringes, disgorging visitors from the four corners of the world. Their narrow streets are filled with gawking gangs following the raised umbrellas of vociferous guides. You would be hard put to find a baker or grocer but there is one souvenir shop after another, covering the old cobblestones with hideous display stands full of knick-knacks. Plastic chairs and sunshades dedicated to the great god Coca-Cola have invaded the squares. Big blackboards boast of *bocadillos* and eight-euro menus.

Drunk with solitude, the pilgrim feels dizzy amid the clamour of these bazaars. Having met hardly anyone on the Camino, he is astonished to see so many people wearing scallop shells and other Compostela signs and symbols. Of course there are a few genuine pilgrims among them. But the great majority wear leather moccasins or espadrilles. Their fresh faces and smart, clean clothes are hardly compatible with the rigours of the Way. As you watch them returning to their coaches you realise that they belong to the category of motorised pilgrims. Tour operators have sold them Compostela and are taking them there, stopping off briefly at places "of interest".

The pedestrian pilgrim has no right to get incensed about all this. After all, the coach tours make the pilgrimage accessible to people who may be too old or too busy to walk for a thousand kilometres. But, leaving aside value judgements, there is no doubt that the presence of these crowds is an obstacle to the peaceful contemplation of ancient monuments. Walkers in Cantabria find themselves on the horns of a dilemma: they can either have all the silence and solitude they want by going through charmless landscapes and along endless dreary roads, or they can gaze upon architectural wonders that are barely visible through the hordes of baying humanity for whom the camcorder has replaced the eye, and the coach the legs.

I fled. Santillana del Mar, "the most beautiful village in Europe", according to Jean-Paul Sartre (what was he doing there?) detained me for ten minutes, time to drink an orange juice on a restaurant patio. None of the waitresses I asked knew anything about the place. Recruited for the summer season, they all came from elsewhere. A medical conference added its crowds and buses to the already dense mass of tourists and motorised pilgrims.

I was not sorry to leave all these magnificent buildings that had lost all meaning for me, now that they had become a mere backdrop for a modern tragedy called mass tourism.

As soon as I had got back to the silence of the Way, I felt like I had escaped a shipwreck. The tranquil beauty of the countryside beyond Santillana enhanced the contrast. At the very top of a hill stood a deserted *ermita*,[1] a welcome balm to the eyes after the crowds in the village. Perhaps the hermits had once shared my confusion and my need to escape the bustling crowds. The spirit of the Way is surely there, in the wish to wander through the world in order to escape it and to find others where there is nobody. "Men," wrote Alphonse Allais, "like to congregate in deserts."

Comillas is not quite so full of tourists but Gaudí's famous Capricho pulls in the crowds, and I only managed to find some

1 A small church or chapel, often providing shelter for pilgrims in the Middle Ages.

peace by lying down on the vast, empty lawns around the neo-Gothic buildings of the Pontifical University.

As for Colombres, it is the epicentre of the region from where the Spaniards who had set off to seek their fortunes in South America built their palaces on their return. It was raining hard when I arrived. I took shelter under an awning outside the "Indianos" Archive at the Museum of Emigration, one of the buildings erected by prodigal sons back from the tropics. The downpour had driven off both visitors and locals, and the place regained a little of its nostalgic charm.

It bore witness to another adventure, one which is not part of the world of St James but an extension of it: the path followed by emigrants across the ocean, much further west than Santiago de Compostela, all the way to the land of the Americas. A different feeling, another history, and here and now it had no resonance for me. These deserted palaces seemed to me closer to the empty housing developments that disfigured the towns and villages of the region than to the medieval monuments scattered by pilgrims along the Way. Leaving Colombres, my only regret was to run into yet another main road. The rain was hammering down, and I took refuge in a transport motel. During the night, the sound of heavy lorries splashing up spray served as my lullaby. You can't always choose your cantilena.

Chastened by these bad experiences, I thought I should be able to find happiness in a lesser-known and less visited historic town, which I reached at the same time as the sun, at the close of a rainy afternoon. San Vicente de la Barquera is on an estuary. The pilgrim can see the town from a long way off, crossing a long road bridge. The area around the port is not particularly attractive, devoted to fishing and beach tourism, for which the season had not yet started.

A few scattered tourists wandered under the arcades of the main shopping street. The only consolation they could find were huge portions of ice cream, which they ate as they walked. Seeing their satisfied faces, I bought one and was not disappointed. Licking my cone filled with raspberry and black-currant ice cream, I left the lower town and began to climb up the narrow streets towards the castle. It was a magical place. Well restored but not excessively so, tranquil but not deserted, full of medieval relics, yet lived in and lively, the historic quarter of San Vicente is a treat for despairing pilgrims. However indifferent the walker may be to the Camino's historical bric-a-brac, in the end he'll succumb to the nostalgia game. The pilgrim likes to believe he is following in the footsteps of millions of others who have taken the same route over the centuries. That is why in the right circumstances, and San Vicente provides them, the pilgrim, whoever he is, feels the stones around him vibrating with history. He will find unparalleled joy in letting his imagination play tricks with him, muddling up different epochs, pretending he is back in the time of *The Name of the Rose*. Unlike the necrotic towns along the route through

Cantabria, the citadel of San Vicente is a place that is very much alive, one in which the present is transformed into eternity. Long after I had finished my ice cream, I was still wandering around, lost in the charm of this wonderful town. It was starting to get late. I decided to look for somewhere to stop for the night, among these whispering walls.

16

In the Guru's Lair

It was then that I spotted a private hostel in a building close to the old town hall. The entrance wasn't on the street but below it, via a garage in the basement. Rows of walking boots, neatly lined up on racks, indicated that I had now entered the kingdom of smelly feet, one of whose subjects I was and, in this particular aspect, not the least. I added my faithful companions from Guernica to the diverse collection of boots on display and went inside.

The first, rather large room was filled by a huge, long table. The walls were studded with countless postcards, photos and newspaper cuttings, long faded if not by the sun – which could never penetrate this cellar – then by the oxygen, scarce though it was down here.

The nauseating smell of some sort of food wafted in through the open door of a kitchen. Two or three pilgrims of different origins, mainly German, crossed the room while I stood waiting for the *hospitalero* to appear. My Teutonic fellow pilgrims greeted me amiably and, to establish a true complicity between us, ostentatiously sniffed the air, which stank of stale fat, making appreciative "Mmmm!" noises. Their indulgence was astounding and also made it all too clear that whatever was cooking was not destined for the dog chained up at the garage door but for us.

At that moment a young man emerged from Gargamel's lair and headed towards me. He demanded five euros (the price of an overnight stay) and my *credencial* and watched me with contempt while I rummaged in my rucksack. His whole manner reminded me of one of the two main characters in the powerful and horrifying American novel *Mandingo*. It features a father and son, who keep a farm in the Deep South where they raise humans. Their "cattle" are slaves whom they fatten up and force to reproduce so they can sell their offspring to plantation owners. The son, despite his tender age, had become used to treating these human beings as beasts, chaining them up and beating them without the slightest trace of empathy. Just for a moment I wondered if my young jailer was not about to inspect my teeth . . .

Once I had paid my dues, the youth led me into a dark tunnel and opened a door. In what must once have been a garage or cellar, bunks had been arranged so close together that it was scarcely possible to move between them. Shoving aside some Dutch and Korean guests, who were standing there in their shirtsleeves, he led me to a bed which he pointed at. Then he turned on his heels and left me to my fate.

With its dim lighting, its low ceiling criss-crossed with pipes, and yellowing plaster, the place reminded me irresistibly of the post office in Sarajevo during the Bosnian war. Occupied by troops of various nationalities from the UN protection force, this building, divided up with temporary partitions, was the kingdom of camp beds, camping showers and combat rations. To be quite honest, I have to say the Blue Helmets were more comfortably lodged.

I put my rucksack down on my allotted mattress. It made a deep hollow, giving me a good idea of how much the worn-out springs would sag beneath my weight. The bunk below was occupied by a cyclist who was sitting on the edge of his bed and rubbing cream into his callused feet. It was hard to decide which smelled worse, the velocipedist's feet, or the brown ointment he was covering them with. The man greeted me with a "*Bon Camino*", somewhat inappropriately, since the only path open to me at that moment was the one to the upper bunk. A certain nasal tone in his voice made me suspect two things: that he was German, which was fine with me, but more importantly that he belonged to the vast international brotherhood of snorers.

I decided to take advantage of my stay in this hostel by at least taking a shower. The washrooms were hidden in another corner of the building, hardly any better lit. To prevent pilgrims indulging in excessive water consumption, the traditional taps had been replaced with the push-down variety. Pressing hard on the metal button – which became impossible once you had soapy hands – released a brief torrent of lukewarm water, which then immediately dried up. Never before had I seen such a sophisticated piece of experimental hardware for artificially inducing pneumonia. Fortunately, after a few minutes' detention, I had acquired the rebellious spirit shared by all prisoners, and I developed a system for jamming the pushbutton with the help of a cotton bud. I will gladly show you how it is done, should fate ever lead you to such extremes. Washed and shaved, teeth cleaned, I found sufficient strength to plan my escape.

I got dressed and went into the main room to reclaim my *credencial*. It was now full of precious stamps and I was proud of it. As one advances further along the Way, cherishing this precious document becomes almost an end in itself; there was no question of abandoning it in my flight. The room seemed vast and bright compared to the dark tunnels from which I had emerged. Enthroned at the head of the great table was a man of mature age with sharp eyes and a stern appearance. I recognised him as the father of the young boy who had "welcomed" me – I have not managed to find another word. By his whole manner, the man made it quite clear that he ruled this realm. Whoever entered must relinquish free will along with his walking boots and wait upon the pleasure of the guru. He questioned me in several languages, knowing full well that I was French from the *credencial* he held in his hand. I understood that this was a way of showing that his empire, like Alexander's, spread to the four corners of the earth and, to put it simply, he'd seen it all in his time.

"Parisian?" he asked me finally.

I could not deny the evidence: my address was written in big letters in the *credencial*.

"I lived in Paris, too, back in the day," he confided to me, without taking his eyes off me. "In Passy."

"Λ nice area," I commented, rather inanely.

"An area for the rich!" he replied. "But I was not one of them. I lived in a *chambre de bonne*."

To keep my composure, I was about to reply "you must have had a good view" but I quickly swallowed my thoughts about six floors without a lift, feeling dimly that he might think I was being ironical. "You also live in a nice area," continued the sole master after God, "but certainly not in a *chambre de bonne* . . ."

I shifted from one foot to the other. The situation was more critical than I had feared. It was very clear that the Great Leader of this place did not practise the discretion employed by pilgrims. He wanted to know everything, and if this interrogation went on much longer I risked admitting to unpardonable faults. I imagined the effect that words like "doctor" or "writer" would produce. I thought of my grandfather when he was deported in 1943. For him, being looked upon favourably by his jailers was a matter of life and death. This comparison brought me back to my senses, and I considered the enormous difference between the two situations. My grandfather was a prisoner, and it was wartime. As far as I knew I was still free and, unlike Sarajevo, San Vicente de la Barquera was not being bombarded. A leap of pride brought me back to my senses.

"I would like you to return my *credencial,* please."

The man was not used to opposition. His guests not only conformed to his rules but seemed to quite enjoy it. I know restaurants in Paris where certain powerful and arrogant men, generally accustomed to giving orders, derive masochistic pleasure from being bullied by a rude and haughty *patron.* The mental whipping they get over lunch seems to reinvigorate them, giving them fresh energy to go back and torment their subordinates in the afternoon. These pleasures are unknown to me, probably because I do not like to take or give orders, and the basement guru must have realised this.

He tried a delaying tactic.

"What's the hurry?" he asked, pointing with his chin towards a register with a pile of *credenciales* on it. "You'll get it back once it's been registered."

This feeble attempt to detain me was doomed to failure and he knew it. From then on we both followed the tacit rules of a choreography intended to avoid any incident. I went back to the dormitory and collected my rucksack. The hostel boss had left his throne for a moment when I crossed the main room which was now empty. Quick as a flash I grabbed my *credencial,* which had been left with the others, and headed for the shoe room. I quickly tied up my laces and was out of there. I took a deep breath and climbed up to the terraces around the castle. The good thing about fresh air and ancient stones is that they immediately make you forget that enclosed, ugly, suffocating places exist. I had definitely been right to flee. Not because my hasty judgement of this hostel was necessarily fair. Indeed, some pilgrims whom I met later told me that it was actually one of the best places they had stayed in. The man I had taken for a guru had, it seemed, turned out to be full of the joys of life, and entertained his guests with singalongs till late in the evening. So I had doubtless lost something, but in my eyes I had saved the essential: the nostalgic poetry of this memorable place which required solitude rather than folksy sing-songs.

But my desertion did not go unpunished: I found nowhere else to stay, banning myself from enjoying the comfort of a hotel and avoiding temptation as I walked past a bed and breakfast even though it was called Galimard, almost the same as my publisher. Night was falling. I decided to put up my tent more or less at random but, since we were still in Cantabria, the best that chance could offer me was a grassy slope beside a motorway.

I got out my camping stove and cooked up a very modest meal. Then I fell asleep under my thin canvas, lulled by the rumble of heavy lorries.

17

Farewell to the Coast

I owe my best memories of Cantabria to moments when I got
lost. One rainy day, I took a wrong turning at a junction on the
path and ended up in the mountains. If I had stuck to the main
path I would have stayed down on the plain, walking along the
roads. Instead I found myself scrambling up a long slope
through dense undergrowth glistening in the rain. Right at the
top I came out onto a ridge planted with spruce and eucalyptus.
Every now and then the wind would disperse the mists to reveal
the coast far below. From up here the road was no more than
a pretty black snake slithering across green meadows – far
off, silent, at last! On the other side, towards the interior, gaps
in the clouds gave glimpses of high black mountains. Between
two squalls I suddenly saw the magnificent Picos de Europa
and realised how near they were. They gave me a hint of another
Cantabria, one I would like to get to know better one day, a
Cantabria that, sadly, the *Camino del Norte* does not reveal. On
that morning I came to know the happiness of being lost in
nature, with no scallop shells to guide me, no noise of lorries,

no deserted housing estates. I found my way like mountain people do, by taking in all my surroundings at once, as you have to when you trace your own route through hills and dales, proud of having lifted the shackles of the Camino from my shoulders. After a long descent through the woods, I found myself in a sleepy little village. The only sign of life was a café-cum-general store where I dried off and devoured an ample sandwich.

A wrinkled customer with a grey bun, dressed all in black, asked me if I was from France. She spoke perfect French, with an accent that merged Parisian cockiness with rough Spanish sounds. She told me she missed her old neighbourhood of Batignolles. Throughout the thirty years she had lived there she had never stopped dreaming of her village at the foot of the mountains. And now that she was back here, the métro, place Clichy and the Auvergnat cafés haunted her nights.

I brought her a breath of Parisian air, and she made me talk about all the places she knew, and how they had changed. Thus I played the of role of pilgrims in the Middle Ages, disseminating news, linking different worlds.

Then, taking up her basket filled with loaves of bread and bottles of red wine, my Parisian friend from Cantabria vanished into the rain, holding in her heart the pearls of nostalgia she had got from me.

*

The nearer I got to Asturias, the steeper the cliffs became. In a thunderstorm it sometimes looked a little like some parts of the Scottish coast, with their black rocks and lush green pastures above the foaming waves. It was as if the sea, sensing that I would soon depart, was displaying all its charms to leave me with a good memory. Having paid scarcely any attention to it when it was calm and monotonous, I now looked at in awe. I cherished its presence so much that I pitched my tent close to the shore. I spent some of my most memorable nights on stormy headlands lashed by spray, with gales blowing all around. I enjoyed twilights filled with golden mist and dawns calm after a storm, purple as a newborn baby's lips. I always slept lightly on those nights, listening to the dogs barking on farms in the distance, and the murmur of the breaking waves close beside me, as the sea continued relentlessly its age-old conspiracy against the land.

As I walked along the last stages of the Way on the coast, I found the wild beauty of the shore so captivating that I kept hurrying back to it. I passed swiftly through the towns, paying no attention to their supposed charms. I had already had my fill of seaside architecture and traditional restaurants, of artisanal fish canneries and picturesque cider mills. I just stayed long enough to get my credencial stamped and devour a daily special for ten euros, or sometimes an "anti-austerity menu" at eight or maybe even seven euros, and then I was off again, following the scallop shell signs back to the shore. I have always had a rather odd relationship with the sea. When I was in Senegal, I used to get exasperated to find it lying there every day outside my window, always calm, always blue, its flat surface scored by vast numbers of dugout canoes. But when I think back to it now, I picture it in the rainy season: Gorée Island lashed by squalls blowing in from the Atlantic, the sea stirred up by the wind's nervous fingers, laced with foam. And I am overwhelmed by an inconsolable yearning.

In Cantabria I experienced the same alternation between rejection and attachment. I was weary of having to put up with the intolerable company of a sea that lacked imagination or, dare I say it, conversation. And then, just as I was leaving, I felt so attached to it that the idea of separation was painful, even before the Camino had taken me away. Those last nights that I spent in the sea's company filled me with sweet sorrow. If I may be allowed a personal comment here, I would say that this paradox marks my whole life. I am certainly not the only one who appreciates people and things most when they are about to go. But I have taken this vice or self-indulgence further than most, to the point where I often leave behind whatever is dearest to me, to find out how much it is really worth. It is a dangerous game, where there is much to win but even more to lose.

Before bidding farewell to Cantabria, I had to face one last danger. On an especially verdant stretch of the route, the Camino passes through an area of neatly mown grass that at first glance I took for an unexpected gift of nature. But I quickly learned that nature there wasn't natural: I was walking on a golf course. Golfers were moving about, pulling their trollies behind them. Something started to trouble me. And very soon a notice told me very clearly what it was. "Beware of balls", it read. I realised that I was going straight across the fairway, completely unprotected. Bearing in mind the warm welcome the local people gave to pilgrims, it occurred to me that some golfers might be tempted to improve their handicaps by cutting down one of these trespassers with a well-aimed shot. I did not calm down until I was off the course, which took me a good quarter of an hour, running as fast as my legs would carry me.

Finally there came the hour of parting, the moment when the Camino left the coast behind and headed inland. This dramatic event took place not far from the village of La Isla, an otherwise unmemorable spot. Separation was slow; for some time I still caught glimpses of clifftops, distant coves, the sea on the horizon. And then it was all gone: the countryside surrounded me. I really was in Asturias.

18

Cantabria: The School of Frugality

Having come this far on the Camino, I had become a fully fledged pilgrim. This condition is manifest in a certain number of external signs and above all in a new state of mind. I have already mentioned the dirtiness of pilgrims. But this is neither inevitable nor absolute. Some seasoned pilgrims are scrupulous in using the showers available in *albergues*. Since they don't generally carry much clothing they must do their laundry daily, a task they perform as soon as they arrive at a hostel. But from the pieces of clothing drying outside, you can see that people have different notions of hygiene, and they rarely wash everything. Just about everyone will wash their T-shirts every day. They fly like banners on clothes lines wherever there is a pilgrim encampment. Socks are the next priority. But other garments are more rarely seen drying, so you can easily work out what is worn day after day without being washed.

The lone pilgrim is obviously the least motivated to make an effort with cleanliness. I have already stressed how rapidly I transformed into a Dharma Bum. The journey through Cantabria had completed this process; I had settled in to self-neglect. Unkempt beard, stained trousers, shirt impregnated with layers of sweat; I felt happily at home in my filth, which protected me like armour. When you are all alone in the world, without home or shelter, when you can feel in your bones the vastness of the landscape all around you, when there is nothing to hold your attention, whichever way you look, when the path stretches as far as the eye can see in both directions, then it is certainly a comfort to walk along enveloped in your own smell, which seems the only wealth you still possess. When pilgrims meet they unconsciously keep their distance. The other's odour reminds them that they risk being indiscreet: two more steps and they'll be in a stranger's private space.

After the charms of the Basque countryside, the Cantabrian leg of the Camino has another merit: it teaches the pilgrim on his way to perfection an additional lesson in humility. At the start, he will have been under the impression that the Way was there to serve him, laid out to please his eyes. Fifty kilometres of tarmac will soon cut him down to size: the pilgrim is there to walk whether he likes it or not, whatever he thinks of the landscape. Concrete pipelines, empty housing estates, hard shoulders, roundabouts and industrial suburbs are all necessary for the making of the true pilgrim, free of any residue of touristic pretension. Knocked about by all these ordeals, the walker will initially feel dazed. Then he accepts his fate. This is when a new phase of the Camino begins: it does not ask for enthusiasm, only habit and discipline. The pilgrim submits to the Way, as he has done from the start without realising it, but this time he follows its orders without a murmur. He has met his master. Every morning, just as a labourer dons his overalls, he puts on his walking boots. His feet have got used to them, and his muscles are relaxed; fatigue obeys him and vanishes after a given number of kilometres. The pilgrim goes on his pilgrimage like the sailor goes to sea, like the bricklayer lays bricks or the baker bakes bread – the difference being that all these jobs pay a wage while the pilgrim can expect no remuneration. He is just the convict breaking rocks, the mule walking round and round the well. Yet human beings are clearly paradoxical creatures, and solitude allows us to observe them closely: the *Jacquet* is ecstatically pleased if he finds some unexpected freedom in the depths of his servitude.

The convict rejoices when he is unchained for a moment; the mule is very pleased if for once he is led down a straight path. Similarly, condemned to the worst, the pilgrim finds delight in the smallest consolation. A ray of sunshine dries him a little as he walks through puddles, soaked to the skin: he beams with happiness. He stops in some dreadful-looking snack bar at a service station and – oh joy! – the ham is delicious, the bread fresh: he is ecstatic. He finds a tree to shade him from the midday sun, and there is a sturdy gate to protect him from the dogs barking furiously in the farm behind him: he closes his eyes in bliss. Cantabria teaches frugality and forces the pilgrim to make better use of his senses to discover, on the surface of pitiless reality, the sweet breezes of happiness and each unexpected flower of kindness.

One day, after an interminable walk along a straight road, sweltering in the heat, I went into a little town hall to collect my stamp. The experienced pilgrim knows that he must first feed his *credencial* before he fills his stomach.

All the offices were deserted, with stacks of paper piling up in them. The further I went down the corridors, with my rucksack on my back, the more out of place I felt. Then suddenly I found one of the staff. She was confused. She explained that pilgrims never stopped there, and they didn't have a stamp for them. I apologised and prepared to make my escape. But she asked me to wait. She rummaged around in one office, then another. Finally she found some sort of stamp and, after a bit more searching, an ink-pad. She then disappeared, and I stood and waited. The stacks of paper glared at me in silent reproach for soiling their beautiful offices with my dirty feet and sweat-soaked T-shirt. And then the woman returned. She gave me back my stamped *credencial* and, with her other hand, offered me a little key ring bearing the arms of her town. It occurred to me that maybe this was how people treated prisoners coming home at the end of the war. I imagined we were in a Gérard Oury film, and tried to smile in the same way as André Bourvil in *La Grande Vadrouille*. There was something very tender, and yet very powerful about our encounter. For a moment I wanted to hug my benefactor and it is not impossible that the same idea occurred to her, because if a free man crosses your path at noon, however dirty he may be and – who knows? – precisely because he is, it could stir troublesome desires in a municipal employee. But I remembered that I was just an escaped convict. The Camino took me by the shoulders and steered me back to itself.

I attached the key-ring to a buckle on my rucksack. It has been there ever since.

19

In the Camino Alembic

The physical changes the pilgrim undergoes are nothing compared to his spiritual metamorphosis. By the time he is on the threshold of Asturias, this is already well advanced but still far from complete. The walker has already spent hundreds of hours alone. He is approaching the Great Secret, but he's not aware of it, beyond some vague presentiment.

How can this slow process be described? To an extent it is inexpressible, like all mental changes that derive from tests of physical endurance. That is the whole point of initiations. But it is still possible to discern the main stages in the transformation.

When you begin the pilgrimage, you spend a great deal of time just thinking. The absence of all your usual reference points, the journey towards a destination so far off that it seems unreachable, the feeling of nakedness that comes from the vastness of your surroundings, all encourage a particular kind of introspection that only thrives in the open air. You are alone with yourself. Your thoughts are the only familiar presence, they let you replay conversations you've had, recall memories that seem comfortingly close. It is a happy surprise to rediscover yourself, like suddenly bumping into an old acquaintance. Thrown into a place that is new and unknown, empty, slow, monotonous and endless, you let your mind contract into the warmth and solace of its innermost thoughts. Everything becomes intense, exciting and beautiful: memories, plans, ideas. You suddenly find yourself laughing. Strange expressions cross your face, directed at no-one since the trees and telegraph poles are your only company here. It is a well-known fact that when you are walking each footstep acts on your mind like a crankshaft: it sets thought in motion, galvanises it, and this in turn energises your feet. You walk in step with your thoughts, and when they rush and soar through your head you are almost running. I remember that I covered the first stages of the Way remarkably quickly. I was not trying to perform any kind of feat; it was just that, as the old saying goes, "joy gave me wings". This phase is short and should be savoured. For this exaltation does not last. Your thoughts gradually subside, like those high-speed ferries, whose prows lift as they jet through the water, only to sink down again as they approach the landing stage.

After a few hours, the walker becomes aware of another presence: his body. This normally silent tool starts creaking. One after another, the various components of this complex organism loudly announce their presence, start making demands and eventually unite in a cacophony of complaints. First up is digestion, with its familiar weapons: hunger, thirst, rumbling stomach, pains in the gut, all demanding a halt. Muscles come next. Whatever sport you may do and however frequently, you can be sure it will involve the wrong muscles. Sportsmen who smugly approach the Camino thinking they've done all this before will be the first to discover that they ache in every limb. The skin, which normally manages to pass unnoticed, will remind the walker of all the places where something is swollen, rubbing, irritated, torn. These contemptible organs, needs, annoyances, rise up from the depths of the body and end up occupying centre stage. They interrupt the merry dance of images and dreams to which you had surrendered when you started.

The pilgrim needs to assert himself and take decisive action. To silence the demands from the lower ranks – to which he nonetheless has to find practical answers – he decides he must force himself to start thinking purposefully. It is time for some serious reflection.

So far, his mental activity has just made him happy. Having contented himself with whatever happened to cross his mind, the walker now has to deal with important questions in a methodical manner. We all have our own store of awkward subjects, and they may vary in number but there are always too many: decisions endlessly postponed, projects we've neglected, metaphysical questions that we are frightened to face.

There then begins a period of concentration, varying in length depending on each individual, when you force yourself to think clearly. I did not manage to stick to this for long. You soon discover that it is extremely hard to concentrate while walking. You always have to keep an eye open for signposts, passing cars, dogs, and on top of these distractions there are all the physical alarms, from the soles of your feet to the small of your back, from the rucksack which is too heavy and the straps that dig into your shoulders, to the burning sun on your head. Of course some ideas will eventually come to you, with a bit of effort. Problems confront you, with some clarity. Sometimes you may even see possible solutions . . .

But then you arrive at a village, fill your water bottle at the fountain, chat with a passer-by, and suddenly it all vanishes: the answer you thought you had found, the problem it had solved, and the subject itself . . . In the desolate field of a mind in turmoil, something still burns – but it is just the blister on your heel that you thought had healed.

Once your mind has lost the battle, real depression swiftly follows. Lost in fruitless mental turmoil, the pilgrim switches between resignation and bursts of desperate effort. I remember how one morning I was determined to devote a whole day of walking to the outline of my next novel, whatever might happen. I was spending that day in a remote valley, which my guidebook rightly described as one of the wildest and most beautiful places in the Basque country. There was a village with only three houses, one of which was a bar. It was ten o'clock in the morning. I went in. A beautiful waitress was setting the tables for lunch. She had turned the sound system on full volume, and deafening rock music shook the granite lintels of the windows. The room was decorated in typical rustic Basque style: old wood, copperware, polished tiles. Through the open door a plaster Virgin could be seen in a chapel opposite. The music was so loud that it turned this haven of peace into a war zone. I realised the waitress was indeed using her decibels of heavy metal as a weapon. There was a mortal struggle under way here between this young woman, with her beauty, youth and dreams, and these ancient walls, this rural solitude, this sweet piety. I drank my coffee at the counter, and with a smile the young woman offered me a piece of the cake that had just come out of the oven. She was probably grateful that I hadn't asked her to turn down the music. In the battle that was going on, there was no room for neutrals. I had to choose a side, and I had chosen hers. When I left, I had the music in my head and the waitress's slightly desperate smile lodged in my memory. All of a sudden I saw this valley, which had at first seemed like paradise, in another light. I did not quite see it as a hell, but I understood how one might want to escape it. These idle thoughts took me to a stream that crossed the Camino. Cooling my feet in the water, I felt revived. And I realised to my astonishment that I could not remember a single one of the ideas that I had laboriously explored as part of my morning's work programme. Worse still, I no longer had any wish to recall them.

I completed that day's leg of my journey, feeling almost as desperate as the waitress in the café, but I had no music.

It is in moments like this, in the depths of distress, when the temptation to cling onto the Christian aspect of the pilgrimage becomes strongest. To be honest, I had almost forgotten it, especially here on the *Camino del Norte* where pilgrims are quite rare and the general atmosphere is so secular that few people ever raise the subject. But when the wellspring of fresh ideas has dried up, and you have failed to rein in those unruly thoughts by setting serious goals, when emptiness looms, bringing with it the triumph of boredom and the host of little physical discomforts, then spirituality seems like your last hope. Compared with secular thought it has the considerable advantage of being supported by all the religious associations your surroundings offer, so long as you take the time to notice them. The guidebook you consult before each new leg of the journey never misses any of the abbeys, cathedrals, Ways of the Cross, chapels and *ermitas* that line the Camino. You are almost astonished at having given them so little attention until now. And you tell yourself that this pilgrimage has many tricks up its sleeve to lead you to faith. It could almost feel like a miracle. This is the point when you start eagerly looking for historical explanations that you had neglected until now. The tide of pilgrims who have taken these paths for a thousand years starts to make its mark in your mind and, however little such aspects of the journey had meant to you at the start, you now rejoice. Faith seems an alternative to regression to an animal state, which is now a real danger. To be human would be to know God, or at least to seek Him. Animals pursue their prey; humans pursue their salvation. It is all becoming clear.

Having worn yourself out trying in vain to think clearly, this discovery has a welcome cathartic effect. Now you can abandon the fight without fear. You can allow your mind to become empty, and give way to your body and its needs; you can accept whatever the landscape, with all its changing faces, may bring, from the discomforts of the rain to the burning heat of the sun. You will not resist at all, because none of this really matters. You know that just down the road, or ten kilometres away, there will be a church to offer the shelter of its cool, vaulted nave, the solace of its ancient stones, the mysterious presence of the divine. Whether or not you are a believer, you will let your mind be immersed in this pure water, and you will experience the special kind of baptism that is the manifestation of transcendence within you.

Until now, my membership of the vast band of pilgrims who have walked this path over the centuries had been just an abstract notion. Now it was a concrete fact, a living certainty; I could feel it within me and see its proof in all my surroundings. This invisible multitude has sprung to the aid of the despairing pilgrim – as if the souls of all those who have passed through this place have come to offer support and encouragement, to give him strength and fortitude.

For me, this transformation occurred at the end of the Cantabrian leg of the journey and the beginning of the Asturian one, after I had left the coast and, heading into the interior, was approaching Oviedo.

20

Ancient Asturias

If Santiago de Compostela was the profane goal of my journey, Oviedo was the culmination of its religious section. It was fortunate that the Way's spiritual dimension revealed itself to me just as I was starting to lose heart. As soon as I entered Asturias, I devoted myself to exploring every single holy place on my route. But once you've acquired a taste for spirituality, all these little country churches, Stations of the Cross and hermitages are mere *hors d'oeuvres*. The hunger of a pilgrim in his mystical phase cannot be sated by such *amuse-bouches*. All they can do is to help him to be patient and wait for the holy city of Oviedo to deliver the main course.

In fact medieval pilgrims considered this city to be an essential destination. According to a famous saying, "Whoever goes to Santiago without visiting San Salvador venerates the servant and neglects the Lord." Saint James is a minor figure compared to Christ the Saviour to whom the Catedral de San Salvador in Oviedo is dedicated. So when you reach Oviedo, you have completed the first part of your pilgrimage. Then another journey begins, in fact the only one that a lot of pilgrims ever make: the *Camino Primitivo*, the Original Way. In the early ninth century, when Asturias was protected by its mountains from the Moorish invaders, who had conquered other parts of Spain, King Alfonso II heard that the relics of Saint James had been discovered in Santiago de Compostela and decided to go and see this miracle for himself. He set off from Oviedo and traced the path of the first pilgrimage. Arriving at Oviedo marks the end of a journey and the start of a new one. From my own point of view, Oviedo was the high point of my (brief) Christian pilgrimage. I found the Camino on the approaches to this city beautiful and inspiring, quite different from the first, profane stages and those that would follow.

Everything came together to make this stretch of the Camino appealing. I was getting away from Cantabria and the coast, which until then had been my guide and reference. Leaving behind this seaside safety rail made me feel proud, like a toddler taking his first steps without the helping hand of an adult. The mystery of these strange lands, even when diminished by all the Camino signposting, was more exciting than the long litany of coves and beaches.

And then I fell under the spell of Asturias. The Camino there is marked out as carefully as in the Basque country, and it takes the walker well away from the main roads, leading him once more down ancient *calzadas*. I was immediately struck by something harsh and primordial but at the same time grand

and dignified in Asturias. For me this was symbolised by the little buildings known as *hórreos* that you see everywhere. The origin of these *hórreos* is lost in the depths of time (they are said to go back to the Neolithic period) but we know they were originally used as granaries. They are raised on stone or wooden pillars crowned by wide, flat stones to prevent rodents getting to the grain stored above. Early *hórreos* were often thatched and surrounded by verandas where herbs, spices and flowers were dried.

These humble *hórreos* have often been disfigured by concrete steps, roofs of tiles or corrugated iron, and windows. Many have been transformed into garages, chicken coops or barns. Yet they remain, still recognisable in spite of their disguises. And some, perfectly preserved, stand proudly on their stone legs, bearing witness to thousands of years of history. This rustic simplicity makes a happy contrast with the sophisticated and, it is to be hoped, ephemeral, pretensions of the housing and holiday estates that blight the coast.

In the splendour of this mountainous setting, all the associations with Saint James and all the places of worship are especially resonant. Above all, this is because Asturias has many remarkable pre-Romanesque churches, dating back to the time of King Alfonso II.

Some of these churches have been well restored, like the one that adjoins the monastery of Valdedíos. Others are in a dire state of repair. I came across one village church that was so neglected that I assumed it was disused. But seeing me wandering around the building, an old woman beckoned me over. She was wearing a crooked wig, and she had to silence her dog, which, as is often the case, bore a disturbing resemblance to its owner. Having taken out a huge key, she showed me into the church. I was filled with grace during this part of my pilgrimage and found this visit deeply moving. Without the cross vaults developed later, these pre-Romanesque churches had to be built with very thick stone walls. The few openings are no wider than arrow slits, and inside it is completely dark. Although these buildings are above ground, entering them feels like visiting a catacomb. The walls are not carved but painted with frescoes which imitate the columns and windows that the walls lack. In the weak beam of the torch that my guide was brandishing, I glimpsed bearded faces, parts of robes, eagle's wings and the horns of a bull. These figures traced in ochre on a rough surface were like something you might find in a cave rather than a church. Though I knew that their inspiration came from the Gospels, they looked much older than their thousand years. They seemed to belong to a more distant, prehistoric past, like the *hórreos*. In Asturias, Christianity reveals unexpectedly deep roots, which connect it to the most primordial forms of spirituality. All this only deepened my fascination for that religion.

A staircase, probably from the seventeenth century, had been added to the building, leading up to the belfry. I asked my guide when this regrettable alteration had been made, and she replied that it was certainly very old. And to prove her claim, she added "It was there when I was born." Then she told me her age. It was the same as mine. I suddenly felt rather glum.

With her ill-fitting wig, jerky movements and unsteady steps, the poor woman was not in good shape. She added to the decay of the place itself, and thanks to her this visit was turning into a painful intimation of mortality. The triumphant figure of the resurrected Christ became all the more compelling. I felt a strong desire to throw myself at the feet of the cross and implore God to grant me the grace of health in this world and eternal life in the next. I was thus in the same position as men of the Middle Ages, and especially pilgrims, who, worn out with hardship and the trials of their journey, could only regain some hope in the warm, welcoming darkness of sanctuaries like this one.

My guide did not spare me a single nook or cranny of her church. Sometimes she was helped by a naked bulb hanging from a wire, turned on by a big Bakelite switch with a creak and a hollow clunk that reminded me of my childhood. The only movement the woman executed with remarkable agility was a little gesture as we came out of the building. She held her open palm towards me to receive a few coins, which swiftly disappeared into the dark, and probably pre-Romanesque, folds of her embroidered apron. Before we parted, I asked her whether the church was still consecrated. She told me the parish priest said Mass there every Sunday. And, with a glimmer of the pride that must have lit up her whole life, she told me this priest was her brother.

21

Bacchus and Saint Paul

In the space of just a few kilometres, Asturias offers a striking contrast between a rustic, primitive and humble form of Christianity and the pomp and splendour of wealthy monasteries. In Valdedíos, monks who could have walked straight out of a painting by Zurbarán were chanting Vespers in the golden glow of a wonderful Baroque altar. Compared to the unrefined piety of the country church, with its old priest and his infirm sister, this scene seemed to belong to a different religion. But that is precisely the power of Christianity – to accommodate two such contrasting forms of spirituality. Between the monks in their holy castle that we call an abbey, and the plebeian country priests with their simple little churches that have more in common with a hay barn than a cathedral, the same symbols and the same rituals have built a solid bridge. Over the centuries, Christianity has given Europe its power and grandeur but often at the price of complete social inertia, perpetuating a hierarchy supposedly ordained by God. Everyone has their allotted place. By postponing all change to an afterlife when the last shall be the first, by encouraging people to endure injustice while waiting for God's last judgement, the Christian order spread a fine net across Europe, especially over the intensely Catholic Spain of the *Reconquista*, where everyone, whatever they did, was caught like a fish. And then that net was rent asunder. Reason, progress, liberty emerged and produced our own disenchanted, materialist world, in which we are all supposedly equal, and completely free to exploit our fellow men and women.

Pilgrimage offers a unique chance to rediscover the vestiges of the lost world of a triumphant Christianity and to experience what it once was. From shrine to hermitage, from monastery to chapel, the walker can enjoy the illusion that nothing has changed.

At the same time, you become aware, almost physically, that this veil of piety, the Christian web that enveloped Europe for so long, had merely covered over places and people who in fact had lost none of their paganism. Most of the religious buildings consecrated to the glory of Christ were built on the sites of much older shrines, some of which are prehistoric. Archaeological excavations confirm that there were once places of worship – Roman, Celtic or Neolithic – where a church or a roadside Calvary now stands. But the pilgrim knows this without being told. When you are on foot, you can sense the telluric presences, the magical auras, the spiritual emanations from a hidden spring in the depths of a valley or on a rocky peak rising out of a forest. When you go down into a gorge or ascend to some promontory, you feel a shudder of that holy terror which would have been so much stronger in the times when men walked naked, menaced by wild beasts, lightning and plagues. And in such places as these, that seem the natural home of spirits of the earth and air, you are not surprised to come across Christian buildings, the final link in the long chain of sanctuaries where, with danger all around, men came to beseech the elements for mercy.

It is through experiences like these that I came to appreciate the enormously liberating role that Christianity initially played, before sometimes being changed into an instrument of oppression. In contrast to primitive religions, which only expressed man's fear of the gods and paid them tribute to ensure they would be benevolent, Christianity emerged as a powerful instrument given to humans to vanquish death. Christ, in the light of his resurrection, is a sword brandished over believers to defend them against nature. He gives Christians the strength to drive threatening spirits back into the darkness, to scorn evil spells, to brave the perils of the most remote places. By purging nature of the assorted gods who dwelt in the clouds and the mountains, the forests and the springs, the Christian religion in some sense took it upon itself to protect humanity and offer it the whole world. Now humanity knew no limit to its expansion, as long as in every newly explored place men never forgot to add a consecrated shelter where Christ could keep watch.

But the walker may also notice the extent to which the web of Christianity has pulled in groups of people who remain deeply pagan. I had this experience after leaving the monastery of Valdedíos.

The path now wound up into the mountains. There was a beautiful view of the buildings, and from above the abbey church looked like a place of peace and harmony at the bottom of its lush, green valley. Having reached the summit, I found myself beside a trunk road full of lorries. I had hardly lost sight of the church of Valdedíos, when I spotted a transport café that also seemed popular with local farmworkers and decided to have some lunch.

The big dining room was incredibly noisy. At every table, men were bawling at each other in raucous voices, their red faces glowing from wine that seemed to be flowing freely. For a few euros, the menu of the day offered a mouth-watering, calorific feast: piles of pork, vegetables drowned in mayonnaise and grilled meats covered in fatty gravy. No-one paid attention to this pilgrim sitting at an empty table by the door. All around, men's eyes were sparkling, their mouths wide open as they gobbled down more food and roared with laughter as thick as the sauces.

Two young, plump waitresses in short skirts were trying to navigate their way through the diners. They held the plates high above their heads to prevent any drunken movement knocking them over. In doing so, they left their posteriors unprotected. Male hands cheerfully took advantage of this, wandering freely. Some, ruddy and black with engine oil as they were, contented themselves with tenderly tracing the fleshy outlines of the waitresses' bottoms. Others, who had gained courage or lost inhibitions through alcohol, prodded and pinched and even went as far as to slap these bottoms so loudly that the noise could be heard above the uproar. The waitresses shrieked, adding to the general merriment. Then one of them began arguing with a man who must have allowed his fingers to stray beyond the accepted boundaries of the game. She started shouting, and the man, grinning all over his face, prevented her from leaving the corner of the room, where she had just deposited a plate. During this altercation, other men standing behind the unfortunate woman launched a cowardly assault on her buttocks, which forced her to swivel around.

It was a violent, savage, astonishingly primitive scene, and at the same time it had a kind of joyous animal quality; it was bacchanalian, pagan. We were a thousand miles away from the monastic silence and the heavenly voices singing psalms beneath gilded rinceaux, such a short distance from here. This proximity gives some idea of the desperate struggle that must have gone on over the centuries between the Christian order, with all its pomp and piety, and the fundamental paganism of the masses. The Church possessed the kingdom, the power and the glory, but basic human nature did not change. Indeed, a kind of symbiosis came to exist between the peace of Christ, symbolised in its extreme form by monastic retreat from the world, and the indulgence of the common people in their simple and brutal passions. The profane were allowed the pleasures of the flesh, of food and wine, as long as in return they bore the burden of labour and reproduction. Thus the monks in the abbey and the waitresses in this cheap eatery had formed a solid if paradoxical union over the centuries which remained intact in this corner of rural Spain.

Only one element was out of place: me. When I spoke quietly and politely to the waitresses, and kept my hands resting peacefully on the table, far from being grateful for my civility, they looked at me with contempt and went off chortling to get their thighs pinched again.

At first I was astonished, but once I thought about it, I came to the conclusion that this was a perfectly natural reaction. People like me, equally distant from monastic fervour and base appetites, are creatures born out of the collapse of the Christian order. Worse still, they are its cause. Struggling against religious domination, these freethinkers were the first of a new breed of humans, proud men and women who claimed to have freed themselves from faith, with all its rules and mysteries, and from primitive instincts, brutal lusts and the rule of force.

These modern beings had proliferated to such an extent that they had replaced the empire of the Church with their own instruments: science, the media, finance. They had banished the old order. And the new one had no more place for peasants than for monks. The waitresses were orphaned from their world because of people like me. I may not have felt I deserved their contempt, but at least I understood it.

22

A Big Slice of Christianity

I had more and more religious experiences as I walked along this section of the Camino. Visiting every *ermita* I passed on the way and attending evening prayers in churches and chapels, I got a good idea of the current state of the little world of Christianity, at least in Spain.

If Sunday Masses still pulled in a lot of people, evening services were only attended by the very elderly. Priests seemed to adapt their liturgical duties accordingly, and I saw some officiants rush through the whole procedure, visibly impatient at wasting their talent on such a meagre flock.

In some places, religious fervour remained impressive despite (or because of) the emptiness of the building. I remember an evening in the Basque Country, sitting in a damp church decorated with little more than wrought-iron crosses. A young woman was loudly reciting one *Ave Maria* after another, rolling the "r"s, and the congregation joined in with a rumble of hoarse voices, like an avalanche of rocks. I could feel the tension mounting with every repetition. The congregation may have been relatively small but the church seemed full of spiritual energy. When at last the priest appeared in the choir, his presence provoked a real catharsis, and perhaps, here and there, more intimate emotions.

Going from one holy place to another, the pilgrim can establish a geological cross-section of the different Christian strata of the country.

In the splendour of the cathedrals you encounter the ecclesiastical elite, the holiest or cleverest priests, those who have done very well for themselves, even if they haven't yet made it to cardinal. These are the ones with the most valuable prebends, the most comfortable dioceses, the most beautiful presbyteries. At the other extreme, in the depths of the countryside, a very different clergy just about survives; priests who live in close proximity to the pagan practices they are supposed to condemn. It is here, among this lumpen-clergy, that the results of poverty, of lives lived behind closed doors in isolated communities, and of temptation are clearly visible. These are also stigmata of Christ. These priests may be incompetents, sometimes alcoholics, perhaps fornicators, but when they are merely the poor shepherds of tiny rural flocks they seem to deserve, if not absolution, then at least clemency. They do not cultivate their vices like the privileges of the wealthy but rather as rare consolations offered during a life of deprivation and destitution. And they are more like Graham Greene's whisky priest than Barbey d'Aurevilly's sulphurous apostate.

In the sparse ranks of these rank-and-file clerics you some-times also come across more modern individuals whose careers remain mysterious. I encountered one of these unclassifiable characters on a Sunday in Cantabria. On the previous evening I had stayed in the pilgrims' lodgings of an enormous blue monastery. I was the only occupant for some time until a pair of Korean women turned up. As soon as they set eyes on me, they retreated to the far end of the dormitory. This was the moment when I became aware of just how scruffy I now looked: after all the days and nights of walking and camping, I must have appeared extremely suspicious, not to say threatening, at least to these Asians, who had scrubbed themselves thor-oughly from head to foot – even including the soles of their shoes – as soon as they had arrived.

The next day was Sunday, and Mass was being celebrated in the monastery chapel. I had been impressed by the monks' piety and kindness when I arrived, and I was tempted to join them in prayer before continuing my journey. But unfortu-nately I let practical considerations dissuade me. The monas-tery Mass started rather late in the morning, and I decided to go instead to an earlier one in the diocesan church, just up the hill.

It was an enormous building, whose stucco was already starting to fall off the ceiling. I feared that one day soon a parishioner hoping to go to heaven might find heaven – in the form of the Church ceiling – coming down to him.

A dozen or so women lingered gossiping in the church porch while I made myself comfortable on one of the benches, keen to soak up some of the spirituality that filled this holy place. The women were shouting now, making fun of each other and roaring with laughter. The hour struck. And suddenly a deep voice cut through the shrill chatter, a beautiful baritone. It appeared to belong to a male proud of his speech organ and keen to show off its full range. I turned and saw a thickset, bearded man in his forties, very smartly dressed, strutting among the female parishioners. He was evidently the parish priest. I got the impression that they had put on their Sunday best just for him. A rather chubby ten-year-old boy, with black hair and a bovine face, was being pushed forward by the chattering women. From where I was sitting I thought I could hear something about First Communion. The priest seemed delighted to include this new member in the flock, and welcomed him by slapping his cheek and massaging his scalp and shoulders. The child maintained his doleful expression and offered no resistance.

I calculated the likely delay with the Mass, aware that I had not gained much by coming here. The monastery would surely have started Mass punctually, and I would have lost less time if I'd stayed there. The priest was still wearing his suit; we would all have to wait until he'd changed. While continuing a score of ardent dialogues with the women, he slowly advanced up the nave, holding the young boy firmly before him. Finally, shielded by this hostage, he vanished into the sacristy.

To my astonishment, he came out again almost immediately, a surplice thrown over his suit. Striding up the microphone, he began to address his audience. Only the Sign of the Cross, hastily executed before he opened his mouth, distinguished the harangue which followed from a politician's speech at a rally.

No homilies, no recognisable element of liturgy, no references to the Gospels; what the priest administered to us for many long minutes was nothing but a discourse without rhyme or reason on current affairs, the financial crisis, the war in Libya, the government of prime minister Zapatero, economic competition with China, the trade in wild animals, the future of hybrid vehicles, the strength of the euro, the forecasting of tsunamis, the value of natural parks, etc.

The torrent of words flowed on and on. The enormous pleasure the priest derived from performing like this in public was written all over his face. He punctuated his rhetorical flourishes by grabbing the boy as if to make him bear witness. So when he was grimly evoking violent events, he would thump him on the back or rub his ears, and then, moving on to more pleasant and peaceful topics, would tenderly caress the mop of curls on his young head. The child remained impassive throughout all this slapping and stroking, and no-one else seemed to find these questionable gestures in the least offensive. The village had clearly offered up this docile prey to the priest, in much the same way as one might toss a live mouse to a python.

I kept glancing anxiously at my watch. Half an hour had gone by, and the officiant still showed no sign of embarking on any of the more traditional elements of Mass.

Comfortably ensconced on their pews, the women of the parish listened, occasionally nodding enthusiastically, even though they probably found most of the verbal bombardment completely meaningless. They had evidently adapted to a state of affairs that they may at first have found somewhat unusual: the extrovert priest's Mass bore no resemblance to Mass as they knew it. But it certainly resembled the talk shows on their TV screens, so they weren't complaining.

I suppose that after his interminable speech the priest probably rushed through some sort of Holy Communion, but I must confess I didn't have the patience to wait. At the point when, having shared his views on Putin's authoritarian regime, he began to broach the tricky question of player transfers in European football, I got up and made my way to the exit. As I did so, I became aware that the priest had paused. He was clasping the child close to him, holding both his shoulders, and using a moment's silence to call upon the congregation to witness his manifest victory over the adversaries he was fearlessly fighting. Smirking, the women followed me with their eyes until I was out of the door. Not without discomfort, I was taking on the role of the demon that the brave and resolute priest had driven from this holy place.

I found myself outside, still a pilgrim but a bit shaken. A fine rain was falling. This was one of the episodes that marked the end of my religious phase. No doubt a man of little faith, or at least one who saw no point in listening to something in a church that he could read in a newspaper, I was starting to feel the side effects of my self-administered overdose of Christianity. Evening services were rapidly losing their appeal; they seemed more like extreme unction. I stopped rushing into every chapel and monastery I passed. And I was loath to make my journey even longer just so I could visit yet another wayside *ermita*, containing the same flickering candle and faded flowers as all the others.

Now I had lost my last layer of protection. At the start of the third week of my pilgrimage, I stood naked and alone, ready to embrace the truth of the Way. First I had cast off my dreams, then my thoughts and finally my faith. What was left now that I had shed all these skins? I was soon to discover the answer, as the path got steeper and the air keener.

23

In the Tracks of Alfonso II and Buddha

Everything in Oviedo is sublime: the churches, the cathedral, the streets, the doorways, the façades. Even the Camino way-marks are special here: elegant bronze scallop shells set into the granite paving stones. The shells lead to the most impressive pavement plaque you could ever find, not far from the cathedral. It is a rectangle of polished metal indicating a major Santiago crossroads. If you go straight ahead, along a little street that winds downhill, you are on the path towards Gijón; this is the continuation of the coastal route. Follow the other arrow, and broad avenues take you on to the *Camino Primitivo*, and you start heading for the mountains.

I had found this junction the day before while exploring the city. When I set off at dawn the next day, the streets and squares were deserted. No thoughtless tourists were there to sully the inspiring bronze plaque with their impious trainers. I stood up straight beside this historic divide and slowly and solemnly took the first step that would lead me along the track of Alfonso II from the ninth century of our era. "One small step for a man, one giant leap for mankind."

The discovery of the relics of Saint James should obviously be treated with caution. The presence of the holy Apostle on the western fringes of the Iberian peninsula is utterly implausible. To put it simply, there was no good reason for him to be there. So a rather fantastic tale had to be invented in which his body was carried on a boat that somehow drifted all the way to Spain to explain the fact that the bones of a man who had died in Jerusalem were discovered three thousand kilometres from there, eight hundred years later. Never mind. *Credo quia absurdum.*[1] Everyone likes to hear a nice story, after all. It is our good right to believe something, even when there is every reason to doubt it. If it makes me happy to think it is true . . .

But this rather shaky and doubtful historical hypothesis turned out to be a political masterstroke. Opening up a pilgrimage route to the west gave a new equilibrium to a Christendom which until then had been largely oriented to the east, to the two holy cities of Rome and Jerusalem. In the footsteps of King Alfonso, the itinerant host of believers,[2] who were driven onto the path of expiation either as a punishment or to keep a

1. I believe because it is absurd.
2. The notion of "masses of poor pilgrims" is disputed by some medievalists, who maintain that the majority of pilgrims at the time were nobles and merchants and that there is no documentary evidence for the vast movements of people that we like to imagine today. See the essay by Louis Mollaret and Denise Péricard-Méa, "Le triomphe de Compostelle" in the section "Histoire du pèlerinage à Compostelle" of

vow, would pour from east to west towards the end of Europe – Galicia, where the sun dies every evening, swallowed in the waters of the Atlantic. And it was not by chance that this surge of pilgrims was happening here: Asturias would become a stronghold that could support the struggle to regain the lands occupied by Islam. Protected by its mountain borders, the kingdom had remained Christian, and thanks to this cunning and relatively innocuous move, the *Reconquista* had begun. Venerating relics was not the same as assembling armies. But later the big battalions of Castile would follow behind. To suggest that the pilgrimage to Santiago de Compostela had sown the seeds for the capture of Granada in the fifteenth century may be an exaggeration. But it is certainly true that King Alfonso set something in motion that would go much further. And Saint James himself, depending on the time and place, would sometimes be portrayed as a weak and

the online journal *SaintJacquesInfo.* http://lodel.irevues.inist.fr/saintjacquesinfo/index.php?id=113 They argue (but this is not uncontested) that the pilgrimage had always been a political issue for the Church. It is certainly true that the first pilgrimages to Santiago de Compostela coincided with the Arab occupation of Spain. The rediscovery of the relics in the nineteenth century and the relaunch of the pilgrimage by Pope Leo XIII was a response to the rise of secularism at the time. The revival of the pilgrimage in 1937 (the year when Saint James was officially declared patron saint of Spain) was presented as "support by Catholic France for Catholic Spain" during the Civil War.

humble pilgrim, or as a formidable horseman fighting the Saracens, which gave him the nickname Matamoros, "slayer of Moors".

I was walking through the streets in a daze, and all this epic history gave me plenty of scope for daydreaming. Once I was on the Primitivo, I imagined myself as one of King Alfonso's retinue. I tried to see things through his eyes, to picture the landscape at a time when it wasn't cluttered up with streets and pavements, houses and shops. The life-size bronze statues of famous people that the Spanish like to scatter around their towns, strange, motionless silhouettes, seemed like witnesses of Alfonso's triumphal departure from his capital, frozen in time. For quite a while, maybe two or three hours, I continued dreaming like this, imagining the banners flapping in the cold breeze as we rode through little valleys, where crowds of villagers came out to greet their king and cheer, and eager courtiers rode in a cavalcade, all trying to get as close to the monarch as possible. I could see this last group especially clearly; my career has given me the privilege of observing these large animals at close quarters. Small cats or savage beasts, all from the same mould since the dawn of time, century after century, they have been trained to flatter the powerful and scorn the weak. And no matter what anyone says, they will always be rewarded for it, contrary to all morality. I'm talking about the eternal and formidable tribe of bootlickers.

But this last effort to give some shape and direction to my

thinking soon wore me out. I lost the thread of the Camino, forgot where I was or where I was going. It was only by automatically – and soon unconsciously – following the scallop shells on walls along the way that I somehow managed to stay on the right path.

I felt strangely calm and placid. The weeks of strenuous exercise had left me in good shape, and all my aches and pains had gone. My desires had slimmed down faster than my body: they were reduced to just a few, some that were easily satisfied, like eating and drinking, and another, that seemed almost unreachable, sleeping. But I had got used to that. I began to feel a charming companion inside myself: emptiness. My mind no longer formed any images, or thoughts, let alone plans. Everything I knew, if there was anything, had vanished into the depths and I felt no need at all to call it up. If some stretch of countryside caught my attention, I didn't think that maybe it looked a bit like Corsica or some other place I had known. I saw everything as dazzlingly fresh and welcomed the world in all its complexity into a brain that had become as simple as that of a reptile or a bird. I was a new being, freed from the burden of memory, desire or ambition. A *Homo erectus*, but a special variety: the walking man. A tiny creature in the vastness of the Way, I was not me and I was not another, I was simply a machine that moves forward, the most basic kind imaginable, whose final goal like his ephemeral existence consisted of putting one foot after the other.

My eyes had been opened, and Asturias now displayed all its charms to them. Those glorious days were like a slow, interminable dance through wild valleys, along magnificent ridges, past unspoilt villages and along paths traced on the mountainsides by the caresses of divine fingers.

There were hours as green as the high pastures, and nights as blue as the steely sky above. There were fresh, pure springs to quench my thirst, and soft, golden bread in village bakeries when I was hungry, and the gentle wind running its fingers through my hair, stiffened by the dust of the path. Everything entered me directly and forcefully, without the mediation of a thought, the shadow of any sentiment, impatience or regret.

I went through forests and along mountain passes, walked above the black, rushing waters of a weir and encountered some enormous *hórreos*, perched on hills like fabulous quadrupeds; I walked in the creaking shadows of giant wind turbines and slept on the crests of rock promontories above deep precipices planted with conifers and holm oaks.

And it was here, amidst all this splendour, that the Way confided to me its secret. It whispered its truth to me, and immediately it became my own truth. The path to Santiago de Compostela is not a Christian pilgrimage but much more than that, or much less depending on how one receives this revelation. It does not belong to any religion, and you can make of it what you will. If nonetheless it was close to one religion, it would be the least religious of them all, the one that says nothing about God but allows human beings to get closer to his existence: the Way is a Buddhist pilgrimage. It frees the pilgrim from the torments of thought and desire, it takes away all vanity from the mind and all suffering from the body, it removes the rigid shell that surrounds all things and separates them from our consciousness; it brings the self into harmony with nature.[1] Like any initiation, it penetrates the mind through the body, and it is hard to share it with those who have not

1. The current renaissance of the pilgrimage to Santiago and its huge popularity owe much to the same misunderstanding. Conceived by Christians, in the 1960s the contemporary mythology of the Way, with its many routes, its references to "masses" of pilgrims in the Middle Ages, and its ideal of poverty, found an echo well beyond the Catholic world. The pilgrimage fitted modern notions of spirituality that were more syncretic and fluid and far beyond the framework of the Church. Many of those who now set off on the paths to Santiago de Compostela were attracted by ideals of asceticism, union with nature, and self-discovery, all of which were certainly absent in the early days of the pilgrimage. Their approach was not so much Christian as postmodern. It could be argued that if Santiago de Compostela had been created by some other religion (following the model of Asian and Eastern pilgrimages) they would have been drawn to it just as much . . . All of which goes to show, if it isn't already obvious, that there is no need to search for a spirituality that is absent in the Christian world in the religions of the East. The Dalai Lama never forgets to remind westerners who want to take up Tibetan Buddhism that they might start by first exploring Christian sources.

experienced it. Some people who have made this journey will have come to different conclusions. My remarks are not intended to convince but simply to describe what the pilgrimage meant to me. I can only say, using an expression that is a lot less silly than it looks: I was looking for nothing when I set off for Santiago de Compostela, and I found it.

24

Encounters

This new condition is not the same as solitude, quite the reverse. Santiago pilgrims who have reached this stage in their evolution are ready to welcome their fellow humans as easily and naturally as they commune with nature. As with everything else, they do so without desire or plan, without illusions or ulterior motives. It was in this state that I had my happiest meetings with other pilgrims.

I should say that in my case this new state was more philosophical than religious. It suddenly occurred to me that Diderot's Fatalist wasn't called Jacques by chance. I felt as childlike and innocent as that young valet, wide-eyed in wonder at the world around him, pondering the wisdom of his master's maxims. With a smile on my face, I started to recite the novel's delightful opening:

"How did they meet? By chance like everyone else. What were their names? What's that got to do with you? Where were they coming from? From the nearest place. Where were they going to? Does anyone ever really know where they are going to? What were they saying? The master wasn't saying anything and Jacques was saying that his Captain used to say that everything which happens to us on this earth, both good and bad, is written up above."[1]

This new mood stayed with me as I walked onwards. Feeling well disposed and receptive to everything and everyone, I was now ready for new encounters.

There is one place in particular that encapsulates for me this new leg of the Camino: the monastery at Cornellana. I had reached it at the end of a long day's walk, which had first taken me to Grado. Perched on a hillside, this town is home to a popular market, and the squares and narrow streets of the old quarter were bustling when I arrived. With a beatific smile on my lips, I went round all the stalls, eager to see everything but with no wish to make any purchases. Then I took a seat at a table outside a café on one of the little squares. It was very hot, and the terrace was crowded with Spanish families, who were all chatting away merrily.

Every now and then they would cast anxious glances at the sky. The rain they feared came swiftly, beating down on the paving stones. I stayed where I was, sitting still and smiling, watching the water flood my table.

It has to be admitted that a Buddhist frame of mind can make you unusually passive. Indeed, you might even end up

1 Oxford University Press, 2009, trans. David Coward, p.3

looking stupid, since a state of beatitude takes away not only all rebellious impulses but also your desire to take any initiative at all. The waitress came running out with a serviette over her head to give me my bill and close the parasols. Her arrival persuaded me to get up. Without rushing, I made my way to the shelter of a nearby porch.

Then I saw two young walkers, a man and a woman, marching steadily along a little street on which there was a scallop shell indicating that this was the continuation of the Camino. The girl looked at me and smiled. She was very beautiful. I returned her smile, quite naturally, just as I might have smiled at a deer that crossed my path in a forest. It was a long time since I'd been as Zen as this. To an outsider, I must have looked half-witted.

At last the rain stopped and I left Grado. The two pilgrims had long since disappeared. The Way here was not particularly appealing: it ran alongside trunk roads and went through modern crossroads. I didn't care. Every now and then there were yellow arrows or scallop shells beckoning me on. I spoke their language. My surroundings seemed like one great big Saint-James-land where everyone was nice and followed their own path.

A bit further on the arrows took me across a river which I then had to follow. There was a towpath on the riverbank; I walked along it and met some Spaniards taking a stroll. They seemed pleased to see a pilgrim, and I returned their greeting with an inane grin. They must have thought I was stoned. Finally, at the end of the towpath, I could see the towers of the great church of the monastery of Cornellana. I decided to spend the night there if they still had a bed.

But when I finally reached the entrance to the monastery, I got an unpleasant surprise. The building was a ruin. Clumps of grass grew from the carved stones of the church, the pediment of the great dormitory was falling to pieces, many of the window panes were broken. Nothing is sadder than a place where so many have prayed and that God has so cruelly allowed to fall down. The discovery came at the right time; I had just left religious faith behind me. So Heaven's ingratitude only strengthened my rejection of Christian rituals. And yet the place retained a haunting spirituality which emanated from the flaking walls and the silence, and perhaps also from some invisible trace left in the stones by centuries of prayers and privations.

I was about to go on my way when I noticed a little sign saying "Pilgrim Hostel" pointing to the other side of the building. And at the back there was indeed a courtyard with dormitories. A bearded *hospitalero* with a profoundly sad face greeted me, wearily stamped my *credencial* and invited me to make myself at home. For a moment I assumed the man was a monk, one of the last members of a community that still survived in the ruins of the ancient monastery. Maybe he had witnessed whatever disaster had befallen the monastery, and that explained his melancholy. And rather stupidly, I asked my usual question: at what time is Vespers?

He looked at me suspiciously. He must have first thought I was trying to be funny; when he realised I was serious he shook his head disdainfully and told me that there had been no monks here "for a very long time indeed". Then he turned on his heels. Clearly I'd got Peppone here, not Don Camillo.

I entered one of the ground floor dormitories that opened directly onto the courtyard. It was empty and impeccably maintained: fresh bedding, individual wardrobes with brightly coloured metal doors, immaculate white floor tiles. I realised that this was a municipal hostel, a rare but excellent version of the pilgrim *albergue*. As long, of course, as the local councillors had been kind enough to provide their town with such an establishment, these municipal hostels, free from the financial worries of religious communities and spared the inhuman cupidity of private landlords, were usually well equipped, spacious and empty.

I had come across one of these before, and a sparkling new one at that, when passing through the town of Pola de Siero. Thinking the place was empty, the people from the association that managed the hostel had hurried over from their homes to open the building's big oak door. The funny thing was that we discovered two Germans in the hostel, whose arrival no-one had noticed. The man sported a grey beard that reached down to his stomach, and his wife's hair was completely white.

Our first thought was that these two unfortunates had been forgotten and we had in fact found survivors of the Middle Ages, perhaps Frederick Barbarossa and his companion, woken from centuries of sleep by our noisy arrival . . .

I was curious enough to check out all the other dormitories and noticed that only a single bed was occupied in each of them. Clearly the few pilgrims who had chosen to stay here could spread themselves out comfortably.

I went back out to the courtyard. Opposite the dormitories were a series of doors to the bathrooms, a laundry and a kitchen. A little gallery offered shade on hot days, with a table and chairs. I took a seat. A few swallows flitted through the darkening sky. The evening breeze was flapping the array of socks hanging on washing lines; the usual sign that the pilgrim army had moved in – even though I hadn't seen anyone yet. At the hour when the chants of Vespers should have echoed through the walls, there was only silence, and the occasional cooing of a dove to hail the sunset. I don't know how long I had been sitting there dreaming when I heard voices outside the courtyard. Soon a little group appeared. I recognised the two young pilgrims from Grado. They were accompanied by two middle-aged men, a tall one and a short one. The latter was talking loudly in rapid, sing-song Castilian. The pure, clear laughter of the girl seemed to provide the melody line which the men accompanied in their deep voices like a basso continuo.

They saw me, waved a greeting and went into the dormitories. Soon I heard the sound of showers, banging doors and lots of laughter. Eventually, washed, combed and clothed in their most presentable garments, the four pilgrims joined me at the table.

It would be hard to describe the evening in any detail. Nothing special happened. All I remember is how fraternal and merry it all was. The young woman, with her delicate features and bright blue eyes, was the focus of everyone's attention. She knew this and clearly enjoyed it. Marika, that was her name, came from some tiny country in the Balkans and had been living for some time in a well-known holiday resort in southern Spain. None of us dared ask her what she did there. The city in question had a worldwide reputation as a wild party hotspot, so we were of course all speculating about the reasons why such a beautiful girl might choose to make her home there. Such fantasies added to the aura of mystery and perhaps sensuality that surrounded a girl who seemed to embody the Camino's femininity.

Above the gateway leading into the courtyard is a strange bas-relief. It shows what seems to be a naked woman lying on her back with a huge bear stretched out on top of her. According to the guidebook it refers to a local legend. The newborn child of the lord of the manor was snatched from its wet nurse by a bear that came out of the woods. A hunt was organised and the infant was found – fed and cared for by the bear. There is nothing in the least suggestive in this legend but the sculpture is another matter. The infant has adult proportions and a female shape, and the bear – though it is a female one – has all the stiffness of a male. The monastery seemed thus under the sign of a strange eroticism: our group of lone men came out of the forest to gather around the beautiful Slavic woman with the same primitive virility as the plantigrade animal clasping a human, androgynous, naked body to his hairy chest.

Her companion, who was much younger than her, was Belgian. It soon became clear that there was nothing between them, bar the friendship of sharing the Way together. Like me, but even sooner, they had passed the limit beyond which all desire and passion was blunted. I recognised them as two pilgrims who had reached the Buddhist stage and that set the tone for our relationship: calm, detached, enjoying each other's company.

The two Spanish men had started their pilgrimage in Oviedo. They had only been walking for a couple of days and had certainly not yet let go of the illusions of desire. The shorter one, called Ramón, was obviously still deeply attached to something that in the old world – the world before the Way or the one that was unaware of it – was known as chatting up. The tall one, José, suffered from sore feet. Placid and good-natured, he rarely spoke, except to make occasional comments in his gravelly voice on the Camino's steep gradients or the (bad) quality of his shoes. Ramón had a considerably wider repertoire. He regaled us all evening with hilarious tales about the Camino, pilgrims and Spain in general. In all these anecdotes, he displayed a touching desire to show himself in the best light. He said he had already walked the whole Camino twice, and credited himself with many other feats of physical prowess as a rock climber, marathon runner and winner of regional prizes for athletics. All this was in marked contrast to his narrow shoulders, spindly legs and big stomach. But he told great stories, and the fact that they were so obviously implausible made them all the funnier. The young woman roared with laughter and Ramón took this as a promising sign. He must have held to the principle that "If you can make a woman laugh, you can make her do anything", not yet realising that both men and women have different kinds of laughter. The young pilgrim's mirth suggested mockery more than fascination. If she was moved by Ramón it was only with sympathy for the efforts he was making to hide his sadness by playing the clown. Ill favoured by his physique, smitten by desire and perhaps already by love, the little man was desperately trying to play Prince Charming, even though he probably knew it was futile. But now night had softly fallen. A single candle on the table dimly illuminated our faces. We sat up till late, listening to the fabulous exploits of Ramón, as he dreamt his life aloud. And then we retired, each to our own dormitory.

After we all left Cornellana, I didn't imagine for a moment

that I would see the four again. But in fact I did, frequently. We kept bumping into each other on the Primitivo. At first Ramón, still attached to his idea of amorous conquest, did everything he could to keep Marika to himself. He displayed a touching duplicity by justifying sudden departures, which could leave him alone with his beloved. He didn't seem jealous of the young Belgian. Ramón had understood that if he had walked with the young woman for so long without anything happening, he could not be a serious rival. His tall companion José, with his painful feet and scrupulous piety, didn't worry him either. He simply tried to get ahead of him, speeding up on downhill stretches, so he could be free, perhaps, at last, at the right moment, to declare his true feelings. The one he mistrusted was me. It made me a bit sad to realise this: I liked the man, and surely my detachment, not to mention several references to my wife, who would shortly be joining me, made it clear enough that I had no intentions towards the beautiful Marika? Nonetheless, Ramón's suspicion made me realise that there had been a certain complicity between me and the young stranger from early on. He misunderstood its nature, but with a lover's sensitivity, he had noticed it. During our meetings along the Way, Marika had told me a lot about herself. She had followed a man to Spain and had become fluent in Spanish. He had left her. She had decided to stay despite all the difficulties. With the money she earned working for a travel agency on the coast in Andalusia, she supported her mother back home.

Every evening they had long chats on the phone. She was a melancholy, lonely young woman, hiding secret wounds beneath a veneer of gaiety. Beauty was a weapon that she would have preferred to hide most of the time, to reveal it only when she finally met a man she loved. But of course everyone could see it, and it brought her unwanted and annoying attention, stirred passions she did not share, jealousy she did not deserve. The better I knew her, the less surprised I was to find her walking to Santiago de Compostela. I sensed her urgent wish to purge herself of the miasma of the tawdry, artificial world she lived in. There was a purity in her that she could only rediscover in the place where she was born, or on the Way. It took me a while to understand all this. When I was leaving the monastery on that first morning, I thought I had lost her. Ramón had woken her up and taken flight with her, followed by the Belgian and José, but making sure I wasn't one of the party. Unfortunately for him, I caught up with them in the pretty, medieval town of Salas, where she had wanted to stop for a coffee in the main square. I stopped there, too, and Ramón seized the chance to get his team back on the road again as fast as possible, leaving me behind once more.

But in spite of all his proclaimed athletic achievements, Ramón was in fact a slow walker and I caught up with them again. We stayed together as far as Tineo, a town built on the sides of a steep hill. There is a pilgrim hostel at the top of the town. But apart from its favourable position, I found the hostel quite horrible. The lack of privacy was extreme; the beds almost touched each other. A silent queue of a dozen people waited to use the only shower. The *hospitalero* was a rude and surly lout, who treated the pilgrims like convicts. Which they were, of course, but was it necessary to keep reminding them?

When I entered the *albergue* in Tineo, I realised that my pseudo-Buddhist detachment wasn't yet complete. My aggression towards snorers and my fear of sleepless nights had certainly not gone. I fled, to the great relief of Ramón, and slept in my tent, ten kilometres away.

I dawdled the next morning and by rights should therefore have found Marika and her admirers on the Way. Maybe I even secretly hoped so. But chance took me away from them. I left the traditional route of the Primitivo.

25

At the Summit of the Way

There are certain women whom the pilgrim encounters along the Way who seem sent by providence. Blessed by nature with many noble qualities, they have dedicated themselves to the welfare of pilgrims. In the Asturian town of Villaviciosa, I spent one night in a delightful hotel, decorated with all the simple charm of a family home. The proprietor could easily have filled it just with well-heeled tourists. But she liked pilgrims. I do not know what vow or promise she was honouring by taking care of them. Several kilometres before I reached the town, I found little flyers stuck on trees along the Camino proclaiming that pilgrims would be warmly welcome in her establishment. She surely knew of their modest means and must also have been vaguely aware of how niggardly they could be: she had adjusted her prices accordingly. And she would hate to offer them less comfort than if they had paid full price. Come the evening, the pretty rooms with percale wall coverings are filled with all the Camino's indigents. In one of them, I spread out my tent to dry between a nineteenth-century landscape painting and a fine marquetry secretaire. I hung my socks over the carved wooden bed-head and arranged my cooking gear on the round top of a guéridon. I am sure that my fellow pilgrims were doing similar things in neighbouring rooms. At breakfast, our landlady clearly enjoyed taking her morning coffee with us all. While getting her daughter ready to go off to school, she chatted with the hikers, asking whether they had found their rooms comfortable and had slept well, and she got them to tell her all about Santiago de Compostela, a place she had never visited. So they felt a pang of remorse as their instincts compelled them to spirit away all the bread kindly provided on the table, keeping it in their rucksacks for emergencies. I am sure that once they reached Santiago, many of them will have offered up a prayer for this woman, or at least spared her a thought.

I encountered another providential woman, but of a very different type, in the little village of Campiello, a few kilometres beyond Tineo. A couple of lines in the guidebook mentioned a grocery shop there called Casa Herminia. That was all it said. When I arrived, I was surprised to discover instead an establishment specially set up to be a pilgrim stopover. But its mission was not immediately evident. Certainly there were quite a few scallop shells adorning the wall outside, but these are often displayed to attract tourists rather than real pilgrims. My first impression was that it was just another typical Spanish village store, with the usual miscellany of cheap food and drink and assorted household items. On the right there was a little bar where a sullen shopkeeper was wiping glasses. At the back, a cold counter offered an assortment of charcuterie and cheeses. You could guess that these would have peculiar names, which were unknown twenty kilometres away. And piled up against the walls right up to the ceiling, there was a jumble of products and general bric-a-brac, including gaudy boxes of washing-powder, dusty plastic toys and bottles of fizzy drinks with sinister-looking contents.

It was hot outside in the late morning sunshine. When I entered the shop, the silence, the dark looks I got from the shopkeeper and the seeming absence of any other living soul in the village made me fear for a moment that I might have crossed the dread threshold of one of those legendary houses of blood, which welcome lone travellers and then cut their throats and rob them. Sitting anxiously at the bar while the shopkeeper was getting me a Coca-Cola, I looked with suspicion at the sausages hanging over the counter. Pilgrim meat?

But all these morbid thoughts were immediately dispelled when a woman walked in. Short and sturdy, wearing a black dress and apron, she emerged from her kitchen, followed by a mouth-watering aroma that came from huge tin saucepans on the stove.

It would be an understatement to say this woman exuded authority. As soon as she came in, the man behind the bar seemed to be sucked into the grey wall, whose colour he had suddenly acquired. She fixed on me two Iberian eyes that would have proudly outfaced any of Franco's henchmen.

"You want lunch," she declared.

She spoke in Spanish of course, but there was no question mark with this statement, neither before nor after. Without waiting for my response, she continued:

"It's not ready yet. Sit down. There!"

Meek and mild as I was after weeks on the Camino, I took a seat in the spot she had pointed to. She returned to her kitchen and I waited. After a while, a new pilgrim turned up, a tall man with peroxide blond hair, who appeared to have had a nose job. He had the kind of muscles that come from long hours in the gym, and he had taken care to display these at their best with a figure-hugging tank-top and tightly fitting thigh-length running shorts. He looked exactly as if he had just stepped down from a float in a Gay Pride parade. The hiking poles and rucksack, incongruous though they looked, showed that he was indeed a pilgrim, and his presence here confirmed this.

The woman came back out of the kitchen, ordered him to sit opposite me and proclaimed:

"It's almost ready."

We started chatting but in low voices, so as not to disturb her. Having tried various languages, we found that we had one in common: he was Dutch and had learned French in Belgium.

Still full of prejudices, I thought this must be his first time on the Camino, and that he couldn't have come far, given how neat and clean he was.

He put me right: this was his fifth pilgrimage to Santiago de Compostela, and he had set off from Brussels. He had in fact walked every possible route. He talked about the pilgrimage as if it were a joke that had worn thin and, especially, gone on too long. He was promising himself that this would be the last time. But the way he insisted on this gave me the impression that he didn't trust himself and that on every journey he had probably made the same, vain pledge.

Then our chef burst in, bearing steaming plates that she placed before us. No choice of menu: we ate what we were given just as we had sat where we were told. No question of complaining, and anyway we didn't want to. Everything was delicious. More pilgrims arrived in a group. We all said hello and they stared at us for a while. They didn't seem shocked by the fact that the Dutchman and I appeared to be a couple, merely intrigued because one of us was so clean, the other so dirty. Once we'd finished eating, the woman passed among our ranks to receive praise. We paid her the homage she richly deserved. And then she sat down with us for a while and told us some of her story.

Her life, she said, was completely devoted to pilgrims. After she had inherited this grocery shop, she had adapted it to meet their needs. We quickly grasped that her reasons for doing so were not religious ones. The Way offered her a commercial opportunity, and she intended to make the most of it. She had weighed up all her advantages: Campiello was on the Camino, and her shop now got a mention in all the guidebooks. But there was one big drawback that she had to overcome: her village was right in the middle of a leg of the journey. Pilgrims would set off from Tineo where they had spent one night and carry straight on to Polo de Allende where they would spend the next. So all she could do was to serve lunches. This activity was certainly profitable – as we would see when we got our bills – but it wasn't enough.

Undaunted, this enterprising woman aimed to turn her village into a stopover in its own right; to offer pilgrims not only a meal but accommodation. She had already converted an old barn into a hostel, and after lunch she proudly showed us round. With the fierce sun of the early afternoon beating down on our heads, sweating like pigs, the Dutchman and I plodded to the barn, which was a few hundred metres away. The mistress of the place, dressed all in black, led the way. Not a drop of perspiration could be seen on her brow. She appeared to be one of those high-efficiency human machines which make use of every drop of water, burn up fuel down to the last calorie and transform it all into energy and finally into good money. The dormitory was spick and span. She got us to admire the bedding, telling us how much the mattresses had cost. Nonetheless, as in all private hostels, the beds were disturbingly close together. Neither the landlady's insistence nor the cleanliness of the place was enough to make me change my mind: I was going to stick to my plan to keep walking. In any case it was still very early, and I hadn't got anywhere near my daily target. My companion seemed similarly unconvinced until, opening a door, he found a washing machine and a drying rack, both brand new. This equipment was clearly essential for him; it was thanks to things like these that he stayed so remarkably clean. It would seem that he had an original approach to pilgrimage: not going from church to monument but rather from a 40°C cotton programme to a delicates wash with a 600 rpm spin cycle. After five pilgrimages the Way must have lost all appeal for him, except for these domestic appliances, judging by his exclamations of joy in the laundry room. Without further ado he filled a machine with T-shirts and socks and announced that he was staying the night. As she saw me leaving, the landlady still didn't abandon her attempts to persuade me to stay. She pointed to the first scallop shell on the Camino and advanced what to her must have been an overwhelming commercial argument.

"If you set off from here," she announced in a voice thick with pride, "there is an alternative route. You won't find it in your guidebook, not yet. But it is clearly marked. Yes, sir, there are shells and yellow arrows all the way."

I showed my interest. A different route meant even fewer people, and up here in the mountains, places even wilder and more remote.

"And from a historical point of view," she continued, now well into her stride, "it's much more interesting than the usual route. You will discover no less than four pilgrim *hospitales* from the Middle Ages. And breathtaking landscapes." She was clearly saving the best bit until the end.

"But it's long. You don't go through Polo de Allende. The first hostel is thirty kilometres away. In other words, a day's walk from here." The logical conclusion, and she paused in silence to let this sink in, was that I must stay in her hostel. Unfortunately for her, I had a joker up my sleeve which I nonchalantly threw down.

"No problem," I said. "I've got a tent. I can always sleep on the way."

The woman finally understood she was beaten. But since it was not in her nature to admit defeat without putting up a fight to the bitter end, she tried to make me, if not a customer, then at least a tout.

"Do take the alternative route!" she whispered to me, almost pleadingly, pulling at my sleeve. "Take it, and then write to them about it. Write to all those people who publish guidebooks in your country, tell them that this is the most beautiful route there is. Make them correct their mistake and recommend Campiello as a stopover."

I promised I would, which was rather cowardly of me. In my detached state, I think I really believed I would do so. And in a way, I am honouring my commitment by writing these lines. For I can honestly say that this alternative route through the mountains is incomparably beautiful and should on no account be missed.

Its interest, *pace* my grocer, does not lie in the celebrated medieval *hospitales* that she mentioned. The first of these consists of a pile of stones covered with brambles. There is a little notice that I suspect she placed there herself, proudly proclaiming: 'first hostel'. Of the second there still remains a piece of wall some eighty centimetres high. The third is much the same. As for the last one, I remember it as a few stony outcrops among which a flock of sheep were grazing. The cold air at this altitude, the exhausting ascent and my thirst must have united to give me hallucinations. I was sure the sheep were sniggering at me as I read the notice.

But if these so-called monuments were disappointing, the journey itself on this alternative route kept all its promises and more.

The path becomes fainter as it climbs. In some places it is almost invisible, just a trace, a virtual line grazing the surface of the mountain. The seasoned pilgrim, trained by long weeks on the Camino to spot waymarks before they appear, must use his skills to the full in wild spaces like these. He navigates by rule of thumb. Mentally, he plots a route over the high mountains, draws a path through the valleys. Step by step he will find his way, work out a route that matches the scale of these towering peaks, a route that he can feel, that he can imagine. Without changing his pace, he leaps over ridges and cuts across chasms. He has never been as small as he is now in the midst of this vast landscape, yet at the same time his mind and the feeble strength of his footsteps make him its equal. The hiker is, to borrow the words of Victor Hugo, a giant dwarf. He is at the height of his powers yet has never felt so humble. His weeks of wandering have plunged him into a state of passive acceptance, his soul is free from all desire or expectation, his body has overcome suffering and tamed impatience. And now, in this utterly beautiful, endless but finite immensity, the pilgrim is ready to recognise something greater than himself, in fact greater than everything. If during this long leg through the mountains I may not have seen God, I did at least feel His breath.

All those churches and monasteries had been mere antechambers where I had been prepared for the coming of something still invisible. Now that these places had made me receptive to the great mystery, I was finally admitted into its presence. Only once the pilgrim is truly alone and almost naked, unencumbered by liturgical glitter, can he rise towards heaven. All religions merge in this face-to-face encounter with the Fundamental Principle. Like the Aztec priest on his pyramid, the Sumerian on his ziggurat, Moses on Mount Sinai, Christ at Golgotha, the pilgrim in these high and lonely places, up among the winds and the clouds, detached from the distant world far below him, and freed from his suffering and vain cravings, can at last attain Oneness, the Essence, the Origin. It does not matter what name you give it. It does not matter what embodies this name.

I had come to a desolate pass, where the ground was covered with short grass. White swirls of mountain mist rolled around tall, scattered rocks. Little lakes punctuated the green of the high pastures and mirrored the sky. I had passed young cattle and little flocks of sheep. Then all of a sudden a group of wild horses stood out against the horizon. They had long manes and were running free, driven by the wind or perhaps spooked by my approach. But one of them, bigger and more intrepid, waited, motionless, and looked at me. And then he traced an arabesque in the air, twisting and lowering his neck, pulling back and up on his hind legs, spun round and, after giving me one last look, disappeared.

Had I been a prehistoric man, how fast I would have run back to my cave to draw on the wall this briefly glimpsed divinity, the embodiment of everything that is strong and beautiful! In the same way, men and women today, after the long detour of different monotheisms, sometimes find sudden spiritual revelations, incarnations of the divine in the wonders of the natural world: in clouds, mountains, horses. The pilgrimage is a journey that unites all the stages of human belief, from the most polytheistic animism to the Word incarnate. The Way re-enchants the world. And after it, we are all free to make what we will of this new reality saturated with the sacred, to enclose our rediscovered spirituality in one religion or another, or in none at all. Through our bodies and all the privations of our journey, our parched minds are refreshed and we forget the despair into which we were driven by the total domination of the material over the spiritual, science over faith and the life-span of the mortal body over the eternity of the beyond. All of a sudden we are suffused with an astonishing surge of energy and we are not quite sure what to do with it.

I am forever grateful to the industrious grocer of Campiello for allowing me to experience this intensely powerful stage of the pilgrimage. As I walked back down to the dam at Salime, I felt that I was no longer the same person. Of course I wasn't returning with the tablets of the Law, no voice had dictated to me a new Quran or new Gospels. I hadn't become a prophet, and I am not writing these lines to convert anyone to anything. But for me this was the mystical summit of the Way. On that path it felt as if reality was dissolving, letting me perceive what lies beyond it, something which flows in every living creature.

A new plenitude now joined my Buddhist beatitude. Never had the world looked so beautiful.

26

An Apparition in the Forest

But you cannot always live on summits, literally or figuratively. You have to come back down again and find your fellow men and women. And that is what I did, making my way through the thick forest of holm oaks that surrounds the vast reservoir of Salime. In the depths of this forest, in the late afternoon, I encountered a strange character. From afar, the first human being that I saw after my descent from the heights looked rather like a large wood sprite. My ancient ancestors might have thought they had met a satyr or a faun, an avatar of a forest god. But as I got closer it became evident that this creature worshipped Bacchus rather than Pan. The man was seriously drunk. He was clearly a pilgrim and, indeed, a quintessential example of the type. It is not uncommon to come across walkers with one or two traditional accessories, like the pilgrim's staff or a scallop shell. But this one had the lot: a cape that came down to his ankles, a hat with a raised brim at the front, crosses of Saint James stuck all over him and scallop shells of every variety, ranging from those you might get in your local fishmonger to a stylised silver version mounted on a brooch. As in the Middle Ages, pear-shaped gourds hung from his enormous staff. The only modern addition was a rucksack with two straps instead of a medieval pilgrim satchel. But even that was an old-fashioned one, in beige canvas, so it didn't spoil the look.

The man's face was half-hidden by a grey beard, as bushy as the forest around us. I halted in front of him, and he stared hard at me with two pale eyes in sockets swollen by oedema. Holding on to his great staff with both hands he swayed from side to side.

"*Bon Camino,*" I ventured.

He emitted an inebriated growl. I found it hard to understand his reply.

"*'uten 'ag!*"

This sounded like German. Scraping together my schoolboy memories, I said a few words in his language. The man nodded, staggered around his staff a bit more, then asked me if I was German. Only someone who was very drunk could have imagined this, given my appalling grammar and my accent. I replied that I was French, and he ruminated on over this response for a few moments, working his jaw. Then he suddenly took one hand off his staff, pointed at me with a gnarled index finger and tapped me on the chest.

"*Du weißt,*" he exclaimed, "*ich bin ein alter Mann.*"

I nodded.

"You know how old I am?" he continued, still in German. "Seventy-eight years old!"

I tried to look surprised and impressed at this revelation. And in fact I really was astonished: how could a man of that age be here all alone in the woods, in this heat, so far from home and especially still so far from Santiago de Compostela? It suddenly occurred to me that he might be ill rather than inebriated. Maybe he had a bit of a sunstroke. Victims of meningeal haemorrhage sometimes show symptoms that suggest psychological disturbance or even alcohol intoxication.

Did he need anything? Could I help him at all? He grasped his staff again and shouted indignantly.

"Nein, nein, nein!"

You'd have thought I was trying to rob him. To prove that he could do very well without any help from me, he added:

"I started in Cologne."

Cologne! Even a normal walker would have taken three months to come all the way from there. But considering his age, and how much he obviously drank, and the fact that only his staff appeared to keep him upright . . .

"On your way!" he barked. "Off you go! And if you see another pilgrim up ahead, ask him if he's Günther."

"Oh, you're not on your own!"

He ignored my remark.

"If you see him, tell him Ralf won't be long. I'm Ralf."

I said goodbye and walked off. I looked back a few times,

and he was still standing there, his staff planted between his feet as if he was taking root in the forest. Then I lost sight of him. I found no Günther on my way. The path emerged from the forest by the dam at the Salime reservoir. It was very hot and I was dying of thirst. I sat down on a restaurant terrace overlooking the reservoir and ate an ice cream. In the air-conditioned interior, a coach load of motorised pilgrims were feasting. I would have been more comfortable there too. But the restaurant dog had just sniffed at me with disgust, and I did not have enough nerve to expose these fresh, clean and smartly dressed men and women to my odour. I had just spent two nights in a tent in the mountains, with no washing facilities, and I had run out of clean clothes . . .

When I arrived in the little town of Grandas de Salime, I walked past the beautiful church with its external cloisters, and then took the main street, determined to find a bed for the night. According to my guide book the main café-bar rented out two or three guest rooms. I needed a shower, a good night's sleep without any menacing snorers, somewhere to wash my clothes. The guest rooms were in a little house opposite the café, where the proprietor lived with his family. There were indoor plants in the corridors and religious pictures on the walls. The small room that was available suited me fine: its window faced west. I would have time to dry my washing in the last rays of the sunset.

I scrubbed myself thoroughly, put on a T-shirt and shorts

that were less dirty than the others, slipped my toes into flip-flops and went out to take a look at the village. To my astonishment, the first person I saw in the street, sitting outside a café, was Ralf, minus his hat and his pilgrim clutter. He was dressed simply in a striped peasant shirt with trousers held up by big braces. Sitting opposite him was another man of a similar age, who in all likelihood was Günther.

Before them, on the little cast-iron table, stood two one-litre beer mugs. The fact that Ralf had got here was another one of those Saint James miracles. But the golden liquid in those two jugs, crowned by a foaming head, had clearly played its part in his resurrection.

27

Galicia! Galicia!

The next day was a special one: it marked my arrival in Galicia, Spain's most westerly province and the place where the relics of Saint James were discovered. And although Santiago de Compostela is the goal of this pilgrimage, the entire province of Galicia benefits from the prestige of the saint's miraculous presence. When you enter Galicia, the destination is within your grasp. Despite the fondness I had developed for Asturias, I couldn't wait to leave the province and embark on this final stage of my journey.

As I've said before, the battle-hardened pilgrim is free of desires. If I had needed to keep walking for another month I would have done so without a murmur. But not being impatient does not mean you have lost your emotions. That's another discovery you make on the Way – the feelings of exaltation, joy and peace get stronger and stronger as you approach your goal. When you were still hundreds of kilometres away, Santiago de Compostela was no more than a name, Saint James only a blurred image in the daze of a daydream. But as you get closer, you soon start feeling its presence. It will reveal itself in a concrete place, no longer one that you think and dream about but one that you can perceive with your senses: you will be able to see it and touch it.

In Asturias, with its high altitudes and austere landscape, your destination feels further away than it does anywhere else on the journey. But when you are in Galicia, right next to Asturias, it seems closer than ever. The passage from one place to another is thus highly symbolic.

I had no idea what the border would look like. It is high up on the Alto del Acebo pass. You get there via a path which winds gently up a wooded slope. Long before arriving at the pass, I could see the mountain top standing out against the clouds that had blown in from the sea. A row of wind turbines stretched along the ridge, black silhouettes against the clear blue, like stitches along the border between earth and sky. Their blades resembled knots arranged on these threads which firmly hold the two worlds together. It was as if a giant had taken a scalpel and cut open the belly of the horizon to reach its entrails and then hurriedly sewn the wound back together.

Once metaphors like this get stuck in the mind of the weary hiker they become more elaborate with every step. The dream only shatters when you reach the summit. Close up, the huge wind turbines reveal their true identity: they are machines. Their massive bases are firmly embedded in concrete. Their enormous blades creak lugubriously. Today's mills have no miller. They belong to the world of H. G. Wells, not that of Alphonse Daudet. Whoever walks past bows in humility. These producers of "gentle" energy are violent, arrogant, malevolent machines. Standing in the middle of a field or on a hilltop, they are intrusive and strangely menacing, as though they had escaped from the industrial world and come to invade nature and subject it to their law.

On the other side of the pass, the Way continued downhill, leaving the wind turbines behind me, much to my relief. What I could see on the distant blue horizon was no different from what I had seen until then, except that it was called Galicia.

During my ascent, I had noticed another pilgrim about two or three hundred metres ahead of me. We walked at the same pace, so the distance between us remained constant. But on the downward path I noticed he had stopped, and I soon caught up with him. He was a Spaniard in his fifties, looking like some sort of business executive, with horn-rimmed spectacles, a Lacoste polo shirt and denim trainers. He stood waiting for me at a spot that didn't seem particularly remarkable. But he pointed at a line drawn on the ground, and I noticed that it began at a concrete milestone on the edge of the path.

"Galicia!" he announced, his eyes sparkling.

He was standing just short of the line. When I reached the same spot, he held out his hand to me. I shook it, but his intention had not been to greet me. He explained as best as he could that we should hold hands while crossing the line together.

So we stood, hand in hand, before the tiny frontier and then jumped together into the land of Saint James. Once we had crossed the border, the overjoyed Spaniard gave me a hug and continued on his way. I never saw him again.

At the foot of the pass I had an unexpected happy encounter. A little bar had been set up in a dry-stone house to welcome pilgrims. The counter was piled up with a great jumble of souvenirs – tankards, pennants, postcards and so on. Every time a customer paid for a drink, the barman opened the till, and a bell on top of it rang with a resounding clang.

An icy wind was blowing on this shaded slope, so I went into the bar to warm up. And there I found Marika and the Belgian, tucking into *bocadillos*. Delighted to meet again, we sat down together and swapped stories.

José and Ramón were no longer with them. The former had given up because of the painful knee that had bothered him from the start. The latter, despite all his alleged athletic achievements, could not keep up with them. With the unintentional cruelty of those who have reached the Buddhist state, Marika had simply stood by and watched as her devoted admirer fell apart. I could well imagine Ramón's distress when circumstances forced him to confess that everything he had said was no more than bunkum and bravado. His big stomach, spindly legs and shortness of breath had overcome the great passion aroused by the beautiful Moldovan. If he was still on the Way, he probably felt as helpless as a beetle on its back. He had sometimes annoyed me, and I had poked fun at him, but I now felt genuine pity and imagined how much suffering must have been concealed by all his chatter.

Marika and the young Belgian were as indifferent to this tragedy as they were to everything else. Delivered from the illusions of desire and freed from reality's enchantments, they continued their way with a new exuberance, for they were now in Galicia.

We lingered for quite a while in the comfortable warmth of the bar, telling stories about our adventures on the different paths we had followed since we parted company. When I mentioned Ralf, they laughed and told me that they had met him several times, most recently that same morning: he was leaving this bar just as they were arriving.

"So he is actually *ahead* of us?" I exclaimed.

"Yes, with Günther, his partner in crime."

This phenomenal pilgrim definitely had a secret. Anyone who had seen him as I had, staggering about and clutching his staff, lost in a forest and seemingly incapable of taking another step, would have found it hard to believe that he could catch up with younger, fitter hikers and even overtake them. Could beer alone account for such feats?

We set off again in the late morning. A pale sun appeared above the mountain crest, taking the edge off the cold north wind.

The Way now led through the harsh, deserted Galician

highlands. The young Belgian told us how he had travelled through places in Belgium and France where pilgrims were rarely seen. He was received everywhere with a warmth that one might not have expected at the beginning of the twenty-first century. Villagers presented him with fruit or eggs and asked him to pray for them when he reached Santiago. Even in the age of television and the internet, the pilgrim still embodies the circulation of ideas and people. We may not trust, or even believe, the instantaneous, virtual offerings of the media, but the pilgrim's journey is an unquestionable reality. His mud-caked shoes and the sweat stains on his shirt are evidence enough. You can have faith in a pilgrim. When we offer up a part of our soul, when we commend ourselves to the invisible forces that control our world and our destiny, who better to entrust with the delivery than a pilgrim?

In his rucksack, the Belgian carried an assortment of objects which he had been given in exchange for future prayers. He didn't seem to believe in prayer and confessed to an ironic scepticism towards religion. But taking his responsibilities as messenger seriously, he would not part with these votive offerings. In Santiago, he would light as many candles as requested and place before them the images, photos or little messages which would tell the saint about the needs of those who honoured him with their trust. Consequently, his rucksack must have weighed around eighteen kilos, even though it contained only a few personal belongings. After two and a half months on the road, what he carried on his back was more like Santa Claus's sack than a satchel.

All along the paths in the Galician highlands, the only buildings you see are small structures with dry-stone walls and moss-covered slate roofs. The fields are enclosed by vertical stone slabs set side by side in the ground to create real walls. These rough, ancient barriers of rock go back to the time of the people who first farmed the land. The walker feels transported to an era long before Christ and his saints, even before Antiquity, to some prehistoric time. A few Christian symbols have somehow found their way to these remote places, but they too must find shelter within piles of rocks and stones. We came across several *ermitas*. Inside, these contained the traditional Marian decorations, pots of flowers and candles, which filled the sanctuary with the faint red light of the womb – safe under the rough skin of a thick, dry-stone roof.

Tucked away in the fold of a hill, we found the ruins of an old *albergue* for pilgrims. These ruins had not been reduced to rubble like the ones the woman from the grocery shop had told me about. High walls still clearly marked out the various rooms in the ancient building. Constructed without mortar, the walls consisted of rusty brown basalt stones heaped on top of each other. Their colour added to the bleakness of this place, through which an icy wind was blowing. But nonetheless it was full of laughter. A party of Spaniards were walking around happily, joking and taking photos of each other amongst the ruins. The men and women had suntans and wore brightly coloured fluorescent clothes. We all left together, and they told us they were from the Canary Islands and had started their pilgrimage in Oviedo. This bitter cold was exactly what they wanted, to get away from the balmy climate of their islands.

A little further on, after walking through a wood and deep into a valley, we came upon a mountain refuge with room for us all. There we found other pilgrims, cheeks red from the cold, sitting around a table drinking hot chocolate. For those of us who had come a very long way, Galicia meant that we were nearing journey's end. But the pilgrims who were already in the refuge – happy, fresh-faced and bursting with energy – gave us a foretaste of the final kilometres, where we were sure to find masses of well-rested people, whose journey had only started in the suburbs of Santiago. With them, the final stage of the Way would become a brief moment of youthful fun, rather like the pilgrimage from Paris to Chartres, which takes just a few days. But amidst all the merriment in the refuge, the harsh and solemn landscape of the highlands reminded us of how much effort the long pilgrimage demanded.

Surrounded by these last-minute pilgrims, the three of us were torch-bearers of the Way's venerable tradition, which had turned us into beatific ghosts, strangers to ourselves, delivered from the constraints of the boundary between dream and reality. Perhaps that is what made us stay together on the last stages of the journey.

Thus we were in high spirits as we crossed these desolate regions. We joked and chattered as we made our way through the narrow streets of villages that were too big for their dwindling populations. Only old people seemed to live in the sombre grey stone houses decked with slate. Our footsteps set the dogs barking, and the sound echoed sorrowfully from the walls as we passed. There were road signs in Gallego, a language closely related to Portuguese. These places that had long been forgotten by the gods seemed to experience only two kinds of population movement – the departure of the young and the return of the old. Former workers from Renault in Paris now ran some of the half-empty cafés, where they sorrowfully reminisced about Les Halles or Porte de la Chapelle. Huge churches perpetuated the memory of far-off days when the village population was large and devout. Villagers look on these grand monuments with a mixture of pride and embarrassment – they are proud because the churches evoke the region's former prosperity, but embarrassed like a host would be when a guest brings a very expensive gift, which humiliates its recipients instead of honouring them.

My companions, who didn't mind snorers as much as I did, slept in hostels. For me, camping out in a cold and wet region like this one was not a pleasant experience. Finally, on the last night before we went our separate ways, all three of us stayed at a small hotel, in fact just a bar with a few rooms upstairs. They were bright and modern, with big windows overlooking a landscape sad enough to make your heart sink: a road without a single car, an apple orchard dripping with rain, a stone shed overgrown with brambles.

There was some hesitation when it came to sharing the rooms. It was a choice between the two men sharing or for one of us to share with Marika. In which case, who was it going to be? In the end it came down to age. It went without saying that I, being the eldest, should be allowed the peace and quiet of his own room. My companions wanted to leave very early the following morning, while I was in no hurry. I was going to meet my wife Azeb much later on for the next leg of the journey. But I decided to get up at the same time to see them off.

We set about looking for somewhere to have coffee. At this time of the morning the roads were even more deserted than during the day and all the shops were shut. In the end, my companions decided to set off hungry. We sat on some stone steps near the hotel to exchange addresses. It was at that moment that a great mystery was finally revealed to us.

A taxi was slowly driving up the main street, looking seriously overloaded. It stopped a little way from where we were standing. The doors didn't open immediately, and the vehicle rocked back and forth on its springs. The driver turned round to collect the fare. Suddenly a door opened and out stepped Ralf and Günther. So now at last we knew why they were always ahead of us . . .

28

Roman Night

Azeb was born in Ethiopia, in a region of high plateaux where the heat of the sun is tempered by the altitude. Her country has given the world some of the best long-distance runners, and people there are used to walking. Although she has lived in France for almost thirty years, Azeb is no exception. She would be more than capable of walking the entire Way. But she did not share my fascination with it and saw no good reason to subject herself to such an ordeal. She just wanted to walk with me for a few days. This was why we decided to rendezvous in Galicia, to cover the last hundred kilometres together. For convenience's sake, we chose the town of Lugo as our meeting point, since it is relatively easy to reach by train. Little did we suspect what awaited us.

Lugo is located on a hilltop, surrounded by Roman ramparts, which in places reach a height of ten to twelve metres. Few places in the world can boast such fortifications, especially as those in Lugo are complete and virtually intact, earning the city the status of a Unesco World Heritage site.

Proud of these ancient surroundings, the inhabitants came up with the idea of celebrating a 'Roman festival' each year in the month of June. During this Latin weekend, citizens are invited to dress up as Romans. The costumes are carefully prepared throughout the rest of the year. Every year, more and more people, all in costume, attend the festival, coming not only from neighbouring towns but from all over Spain. The result is a town entirely populated for two days by thousands of men and women who seem to have stepped straight out of Asterix.

Human nature being what it is, when people are offered the chance to dress up as a Roman, they rarely choose a slave's costume. They are more likely to see themselves as emperors. So it was that the town to which I had come to find my wife was filled with Caesars and Neros. For, as chance would have it, the Roman festival was taking place on the very day that we had decided to meet there.

We knew nothing of all this. Entering through the ramparts at the Porta de San Pedro, as Alfonso II did in 829, I found the place very picturesque. However, after seeing my fifth Cleopatra, I began to wonder what exactly was going on. I stopped a centurion and asked him to explain. He replied with a martial air, staying solidly in character, and saluted me with outstretched arm.

In preparation for the Camino, my wife had been reading up on the Middle Ages, so when she got off the train at Lugo she had the feeling that she must have left her time machine at the wrong station.

Matters did not get much clearer when she spotted me in the market square. For a pilgrim belongs to no particular epoch. This hirsute creature in stained clothing, with emaciated features and muddy shoes, could equally well be from Roman times, the Middle Ages or the present. He was both familiar and unrecognisable. After a hesitant embrace, which made me well aware of just how filthy I was, we sat under a chestnut tree and drank a Coke amidst a joyful throng of skimpily dressed patrician women and merry senators. Rome, as we know, was admired for the harmonious symmetry of its monuments and the eloquence of its orators. But these schoolroom memories are overshadowed by another aspect of its reputation, which speaks to our unconscious: it was the city of orgiastic lust. We had the strong impression, from the start of the Roman festival, that the togas and veils might well not survive the evening. Most of the emperors had glasses in hand before sundown. And the success of these Roman days is above all due to the warmth of their nights.

Despite our happiness at seeing each other again and the desire that we also felt, intensified by my long absence, we could not relax like the Caligulas around us. It is in these first few moments of being reunited with someone who is used to you as you were before that you realise with startling clarity how much the pilgrimage has changed you.

These changes affect just about everything. Of course, the psychological effects are the most obvious, but they are also the most predictable. The pilgrim does not have the same awareness of time as the new arrival, who to him seems restless and impatient, whilst he sees himself as easy-going and placid. This is rather superficial, though – the pilgrim knows that when he returns to the life he led before, these effects of the Way will disappear. However, there is one area in which the transformation is deeper and more enduring, even though it seems of minor importance: the rucksack.

For the new arrivals on the Way, and more so if they do not plan to walk very far, the rucksack is simply that . . . a rucksack. For the seasoned pilgrim on a long trek, the rucksack is a travelling companion, a home, a world on his back. In a word, it is his life. With each step, its straps sink into his flesh. This burden becomes part of him. If he takes it off, it never leaves his sight. The casual way in which novices stuff a variety of often superfluous things into their packs, with never a thought for weight or volume, provokes in the hardened pilgrim a dismay close to horror. For over the course of his journey the walker has learnt how to weigh up every single item of his kit, literally and figuratively.

Before setting off, I happened to come across one of those websites devoted to "ultralight backpacking". I soon discovered that the content managers did not simply proffer technical advice. Their approach was more global, more ambitious, like some philosophy of life. The guiding principle of their thought can be summed up as "Weight is fear". For the adept in the field, it is essential to ponder the idea of the load and, beyond that, the need, the object, the anxiety that accompanies possession. "Weight is fear". And then you start to think carefully. One pullover: that's a necessity. I'm packing two. Why? What am I so afraid of? Is the cold really so threatening, or is it my unconscious here that is weighed down with my neuroses?

Adherents of the ultralight movement go to great lengths in their desire to unburden themselves of every irrational fear. Their websites are full of ingenious inventions which allow a single item to answer several (real) needs. Waterproof capes that double as tents, sleeping bags that convert into down jackets, groundsheets used as rucksack lining. These ingenious D.I.Y. enthusiasts come up with some original solutions: converting a beer can into a camping stove or making a rucksack out of a tennis ball net bag. The site lists typical loads, according to the length of the hike and the weather conditions. You find out how you can travel for five months with six and a half kilos on your back, bivouac on a mountain with a load of no more than four or five kilos, or travel across Iceland for seventeen days, completely self-sufficient, carrying a maximum of fifteen kilos.

I had perused these sites with curiosity and, I must admit, somewhat condescendingly, as they seemed rather weird, a minimalist fad. But I did take a few ideas and thought it was clever to make fun of my fears as I stuffed my rucksack with T-shirts and socks.

But as soon as I started out on the Way, everything changed. The rucksack, to which the Spanish have given the sweet name *mochila*, became my inseparable companion as it is for every Jacquet. This companion takes two quite distinct forms, opposed and contradictory. Open, the *mochila* displays its hidden treasures. On the groundsheet of the tent or the hotel-room floor, you spread out everything you need. Clothes, first-aid kit, washbag, guide book, even entertainment – you can take it all out of your *mochila*.

But at the crack of dawn, when it is time set out, you must put it all back. This disorder has to go into the rucksack without weighing it down too much. In addition to these normal constraints, I had a stabbing pain in my back, the result of an old injury, which would end in a surgical operation some months later. A slipped disc was pressing on a nerve, sounding the alarm every time I pulled on a strap to adjust the rucksack. An obsession with weight soon cruelly dominated me. At each stage I would consider the items I was carrying, but now in earnest, and whether they were really indispensable. The pilgrim who reflects on this has two valuable tools available: rubbish bins and post offices. In the first, he deposits those items he wants rid of, when they are of little or no value. If it is something he wishes to keep, he can pack it in a parcel and post it to himself. So when I got home, I found waiting for me a set of cooking utensils and an alpine camping stove. These had weighed me down unnecessarily, in a country where the cheap and copious *menu del día* appeared to be a universal human right.

This gradual lightening, the stripping of the *mochila*, continued through every leg of the Camino. Reflecting on my fears was no longer a joking matter: I took them very seriously. For example, I discovered that I suffered from a highly irrational fear of the cold (so much so that I could only resolve it by burdening myself for the whole journey with a high-altitude sleeping bag completely unsuitable for early summer in Spain). On the other hand, I was completely oblivious to hunger and thirst. It is true that I never eat when I go mountain running and I function like a veritable camel, contrary to all medical advice.

Without going into any more psychoanalytical detail, I would add that I am highly sensitive to body odour. I always carry deodorant and a change of T-shirts, though I can manage quite well without washing my feet. I realise that these details may not be of great interest to you, indeed you may even find them disgusting, so I'll leave it there. Let me just add that these observations open windows on to the unconscious and we could all benefit from such self-examination.

In any case, along the Way the *mochila* lost a lot of weight, reaching a state of frugal balance which was close to perfection.

The shock is even greater when one is suddenly joined by someone who has not yet gone through this purification process. When my wife, with a disarming smile, said: "Actually, I didn't have enough time to sort out my makeup bag before I left, so I've just put it in my rucksack as it was," I nearly keeled over.

Everyone knows that the genius of cosmetics manufacturers resides in their skill at enclosing a few drops of liquid in a tiny bottle made of such thick glass that its contents are barely visible. For a moment, I was tempted to invite my dear companion to examine her fears, but decided in the end that it was better to be happy that she had the means to keep beautiful, so I shoved the fat makeup bag into my slim mochila.

29

Losing the Way

Once you get to Lugo the journey is nearly over. Santiago was just a few days away, and on this last section the Way rejoins the famous *Camino Frances*, the pilgrims' motorway. This is the most direct route and the most frequented, with hundreds of people setting out every day. I dreaded the masses and couldn't bring myself to leave the solitude of the North Way. My wife, who was now accompanying me, would hardly have a chance to appreciate it. I told myself that it would be a real shame to plunge her straight into the crowds on the French Way, and to avoid this unpleasant experience, or at least postpone it, I gave in to a dangerous vice of mine. Of course I should know better, but the attraction is just too strong, and I can never resist: I love shortcuts. It is a shameful weakness, and my whole family know what damage it can cause. Under the pretext of shortening the journey, seeing a new bit of the countryside or, best of all, simply saving time, I have dragged friends and family along supposed shortcuts that often prove to be both longer and more arduous, not to say frankly nightmarish. For me, such setbacks aren't a problem – shortcuts are an adventure and I always enjoy them, whatever happens. For those who trustingly follow me, these episodes are frequently a lot less amusing. They suddenly realise that the person they are so blithely following is more than capable of getting totally lost. When this happens, there's no point in pretending that all is well. Singing cheerfully when the path has disappeared and you're hacking your way through brambles will only make people think you're mad.

I was of course fully aware of all this when on the outskirts of Lugo I suggested to my wife we should follow an alternative route. Avoiding words like "alternative", or "shortcut", which would have set alarm bells ringing, I told her that there were two possibilities and claimed to have chosen the more interesting one. It was actually a branch of the Way that my former companions, the Moldovan and the Belgian, had mentioned. They had shown me on a map where it started and finished and had assured me that it was clearly indicated. Its main advantage was that we would only join the French Way for the final stage. It was very hot when we set off. Azeb was full of energy. The slow passage of kilometres had not yet worn her down, and she was still at the stage where our standard measure of distance, the famous "kilometre", seemed short. "I've already walked a whole kilometre!" is the cry of the novice, while the seasoned pilgrim will wearily ask: "Will this kilometre never end?"

But behind the sunshine of a glorious day, tragedy may be hiding, like poison in a meatball. A cloudless blue sky, expanses of golden wheat stubble, silage bales wrapped in black and white plastic on the chequerboard fields, a winding ribbon of tarmac ahead of us; everything conspired to make the country-side look benign and inviting. I felt a slight sense of disquiet, which I tried not to show as I led the way on to the alternative route. At first, everything went well. Yellow arrows at regular intervals and scallop shell waymarks all confirmed that my companions were right in saying the alternative route was clearly indicated. But after a few kilometres, the markings became less clear. Again, I hid my concern, and with manly bravado I confidently pointed out the direction to take. We ended up in a farmyard, where two unchained hounds welcomed us with bared teeth. Azeb, who fears nothing except dogs, turned tail and ran. I followed her and made light of the incident – a momentary lapse of concentration, that was all.

At the next fork in the path I chose a new direction. But there was no denying the facts: there wasn't a single Camino signpost here either, and no way of telling which way to go at crossroads or forks in the path. All the paths looked exactly the same, and there was no beacon on the horizon to guide us. We were well and truly lost.

However confident I tried to look, a certain confusion was becoming apparent in my behaviour. My wife, who knows me well, felt the first stirrings of a familiar unease. 'Have you taken a shortcut again?' she asked me, in the disappointed tone one might use with an alcoholic who's fallen off the wagon. My embarrassed reply brought her to the logical conclusion that, yet again, and on the very first day of our journey, I had led her into trouble.

I tried calling some witnesses for my defence. I took out a map and fumbled with what was left of the guidebook (I had torn out most pages during my journey). These futile gestures could not hide the reality: we had no idea where we were. It was midday, there wasn't a soul on the path, and the hamlets we passed through were deserted. We began to suffer from thirst. Finally, we came to a crossroads. There was a tarmacked road with a signpost to a village big enough to figure on the map. Unfortunately, it was on the French Way, and with the obduracy I always display in these situations, I refused to abandon my alternative route. With an eloquent display of bad faith, I managed to convince Azeb to go in the opposite direction. We would get to the village on the alternative route where I had planned to stay the night. Despite her suspicions, she agreed and we set off in the meagre shade of the roadside verge. The road was straight, endlessly stretching up a slight incline.

The trees, at first plentiful, thinned out, and soon nothing protected us from the midday sun. My first lie worked for a while: I claimed that, once at the top of the hill, we would soon see the village where we would spend the night. But, on reaching the top, all we could see was another hill. Not a house in sight, just monotonous fields scorched by the sun. As everyone knows, misfortunes never come singly: we were lost, we were too hot, and soon we were thirsty as well because I had not brought enough water. My intentions had been honourable: I did not want to overload our mochilas. And once the last drop was drunk, panic and bad temper set in. At the top of the third hill, I ran out of lies. The water was long gone. And then the storm finally broke. Not thunder and lightning in the sky above, which might at least have brought some refreshing rain, but something much worse. A marital storm.

I was utterly useless, my wife told me. Why did I refuse to follow the same route as everyone else? I was completely unreliable, untrustworthy, etc.

At a stroke, all my experience as a pilgrim was worth nothing. Apart from getting us lost, my mistake had also discredited my entire journey. Whatever I might say, my brilliant demonstration of incompetence showed that I was no more than an amateur.

We had a blazing row on the roadside. For a moment, I feared my companion was going to strike me down with her hiking poles. Eventually, I managed to persuade her that we should not retrace our steps. She agreed to stay on this route, on condition that we hitchhiked. This was a minor concession, for the road was almost completely empty in the midday sun. So on we went, our only consolation being our raised thumbs.

Two cars roared by at breakneck speed, ignoring us. Time passed, and still no sign of a village . . . And then something appeared on the horizon behind us, moving very slowly. It turned out to be a truck. Miraculously, it stopped. The cab was small and the two men in it squeezed themselves together so we could get in with our rucksacks on our knees. We were saved. But we soon had a new worry: at every bend, the truck lurched alarmingly, and muffled thuds came from the back. It sounded like a stampede. The driver clung tightly to the steering wheel and held course with great difficulty, swinging in wide arcs. Making myself understood in a few words of rudimentary Spanish, I asked the men what cargo their little truck was carrying.

"Three bulls," they informed us.

The poor beasts, panicking at every bend in the road, drummed their hooves on the floor of the truck with all their might.

This revelation left us in stunned silence. Now we understood why the driver had to struggle to stay on the road: these bulls must have weighed at least a ton each and they were extremely agitated. The landscape passed slowly by. It was beautiful, but the main thing that struck us was how many painful hours we'd have had to endure to reach our destination if we had carried on walking. And when we got there in the truck, the village turned out to be much larger than I had thought, and so walking to the centre would have taken a rather long time as well.

At last, we pulled up in the main square. The bulls celebrated our arrival with a final salvo of hoof beats, incidentally suggesting a fresh perspective on the origins of flamenco. Some men sitting on benches in the shade watched us clamber out of the truck. We were doing our best to retain a semblance of normality, even dignity, despite the circumstances. The truck pulled off with its bovine passengers. We were saved.

30

The French Way

I had made a reservation at the only guest house in the village. It was above a café. The owner showed us to our room, a stuffy cubbyhole, furnished only with a sagging double bed and a wardrobe on its last legs. As soon as our host left, we rushed to open the window and let in some fresh air. And there, after getting lost and running out of water, not to mention the bulls, a final surprise lay in store, one that was enough to make us lose heart completely. The window looked out on to a wall, scarcely thirty centimetres away. It might as well have been bricked up, like the windows of a condemned building. It couldn't have let in any less light or air.

We both sat down, on opposite sides of the bed. And it was at that moment that I experienced the deepest depths of solitude that any pilgrim can feel: the loneliness of being with someone else who has not yet got used to the Way.

I attempted one last defence:

"It could have been worse," I ventured.

Azeb turned to face me. She looked worn out.

". . . we could have slept outside."

She shrugged her shoulders, and suddenly we both burst out laughing. Saint James had seen the state we were in and shown compassion.

*

And anyway, getting lost also had its good side. It had taken us through some wild and unspoilt places on the final stages of the Camino and kept us away from the crowds. The classic route to Santiago changes the whole atmosphere of the pilgrimage. Those steadfast pilgrims who have walked and walked over great distances are gradually swallowed up in the hordes of latecomers who – whether they've got here by coach, plane, hitchhiking, train or flying saucer – still want to cover the last few kilometres on foot and enter Santiago de Compostela like genuine *Jacquets*.

There was no danger of being caught up in such a throng on our deserted alternative path. To make sure we didn't get lost again, we had to prepare our route carefully on the map. Azeb, whose trust in me had cost her dearly, insisted that every morning I showed her what she was in for. With no clear signs to guide us, we played it safe and kept to the roads, which, fortunately, are empty or certainly not very busy in this region. We walked through endless woods of fragrant eucalyptus trees, which reminded us of Ethiopia. We only once got lost and then had to spend a long time in a deserted village hunting for a living soul, who might help us get our bearings. Finally we found someone in the little cemetery beside the village church. Two workers were constructing a family vault. Just when we were about to give up, they arose from the dead, or at least from the trench they were digging, and gave us directions.

One of the few people we met on our out-of-the-way path was the pilgrim from Haute-Savoie I had run into in Cantabria. He had obviously not wanted to miss another opportunity to get lost. First we saw him aboard a lorry travelling in the opposite direction and later walking back towards us with his lopsided gait. He'd been ahead of us but another pilgrim he bumped into had convinced him that he was going the wrong way. So he had hitched a ride, gone back ten kilometres . . . and then realised that he had in fact been on the right track in the first place. Now he was retracing his steps.

Our itinerary finally led us to a recognisable landmark, the beautiful Cistercian monastery of Sobrado, whose abbey church is a Cathedral of St James in miniature. The monastery is not quite on the main French Way but lies on a popular alternative route, far busier than the one we had followed. When we arrived there, it almost felt as if we had already reached our goal. It was a friendly, happy place. We attended Vespers in a hall whose walls were covered with modern light oak panelling. The atmosphere was quite different from that of the gloomy churches with their baroque altars that I had visited earlier in the journey. The dormitories were mostly occupied by very young people, usually couples, whispering and giggling. As soon as the lights went out, the man from Haute-Savoie started snoring like a fog-horn, which reduced the youngsters to further fits of giggles and no doubt gave the opportunity for more canoodling in the dark.

When I had gone to buy some fruit in the village that evening, I had spotted the sturdy Austrian woman whom I had met in the Basque country. She had parted company with her friends and now seemed to be having great fun with two young men. With their earrings, tattoos and studded biker jackets, they looked as if they had just come from a rave. No doubt thanks to her new friends, the proximity of journey's end, and the fat joints they were all smoking, she looked radiant. I was happy for her.

We were sorry to leave the monastery the following morning because it was a beautiful and joyful place, and because we were about to rejoin the part of the Way where there would be no escaping the crowds. It was, in a sense, our final farewell to solitude. This was the very last stage – the approach to Santiago de Compostela itself, with all its outposts, redoubts, defences and its heart. Santiago has long since ceased to be a village huddled around a basilica containing the relics of the saint. It has become a whole world, a real city whose presence can be felt from afar.

We joined the French Way in a village. The narrow track we

were following took us on to a wide, well-trodden footpath. But to our great surprise there wasn't a soul in sight. Still, here we were at last on the renowned and redoubtable Way itself, following the scallop shells which seemed bigger than before, though we were probably imagining it. After walking a few hundred metres, we felt relieved but also a bit disappointed. Relieved because nothing had really changed, disappointed because we had expected it to be livelier. Soon we realised why it was so quiet. We were late. There are so many pilgrims and so few hostels along the French Way that everyone rushes off early in the morning hoping to be first in line at the next stopover. On our peaceful *Camino del Norte* we hadn't experienced this battle for beds, nor the race to overtake everyone else, nor the row of rucksacks outside the hostel door, waiting for the warden to start checking in their owners. In the harsh world of the French Way, the place of the *mochila* in the queue indicates the order in which the *Jacquets* will be admitted.

The French Way – sometimes known as the Royal Way – is a victim of its own success, especially on the approach to Santiago. On all the other routes, the few pilgrims blend into their surroundings. Here, they're right out in front. The whole environment has been adapted to meet their needs. Every advert is aimed at them; numerous restaurants, hotels and hostels compete to welcome them; shops make a steady living from customers who may not spend much but keep on coming. As we all know, the cunning of the Temple merchants is boundless.

In these poor regions, local traders know how to profit from the presence of pilgrims, offering them a whole range of ingenious services. Like Mochila Express, for example, special taxis that enable hikers to offload their rucksacks and find them waiting at their next port of call.

When we discovered Mochila Express we understood a phenomenon that had puzzled us right at the beginning of the French Way. The very few pilgrims we encountered late in the day only carried small, half-empty rucksacks. Initially, we admired the extreme frugality of these unencumbered travellers. However, one thing intrigued us. Although they carried little more than the bundle of an Indian sadhu, they were smartly dressed in clean clothes. At first we thought it miraculous, but that was before we realised that it was all down to Mochila Express. These people were carrying nothing, simply because their baggage awaited them on arrival.

On the French Way, the difference between rich and poor, between business class and economy, is even more pronounced than anywhere else. I won't go as far as to claim that this contrast was foretold in the Gospels. But nevertheless, to understand St James's strange destiny we need to recall the story of Jesus and his Apostle's mother.

The wife of Zebedee the fisherman, and mother of the Apostles James and John, came to Jesus to ask a favour: that he allow her two sons to sit on either side of him in the kingdom of heaven. Her request earned her rather a sharp rebuke from the Messiah. He reminded the ambitious mother that his disciples did not make sacrifices in order to earn future favours. In a sense, this conflict still goes on. Saint James continues to inspire two quite different attitudes. First, there is the humble, selfless stance of the poor, solitary pilgrims who struggle across Europe to join the saint in his Santiago sanctuary. Hardship and humiliation are their daily lot, and they endure it because it helps them achieve a spiritual objective of one kind or another. Others, on the contrary – and in this they are closer to James's mother than to her Apostle son – want recompense for their pilgrimage. They seek a share of the power and the glory of the King of Heaven and those who serve him.

In every era, the latest technologies are called upon to meet the needs of those who want a comfortable pilgrimage, sometimes with bizarre results.

As we were walking through a pine forest, we were surprised to hear a voice from above advertising the attractions of a private hostel with luxury bedrooms a couple of kilometres away. There was no undergrowth in the forest, only the tall, straight trunks of the pine trees and beneath them a carpet of russet-brown needles. Nobody could possibly hide here. We were alone. And then, retracing our steps, we discovered the secret behind this mysterious message. A photoelectric barrier had been set up between two tree trunks on either side of the Way. Every time pilgrims passed, they interrupted the light beam, thus activating a loudspeaker attached to a branch.

But we didn't have to put up with such annoyances for much longer, for we were about to reach Santiago de Compostela. Even before seeing the city itself we got to know its famous outposts: Monte do Gozo, Lavacolla, Puerta del Camino, places of deliverance and rejoicing, whose magical names have filled the dreams of pilgrims since the Middle Ages.

31

Final Trials

Lavacolla, as its name suggests, is the place where pilgrims used to perform their ablutions before entering the sanctuary in Santiago. They might have washed their feet and perhaps more in the little pools hollowed out by streams. But it seems unlikely that these natural facilities would have been sufficient to get rid of all the dirt that had accumulated on the skins of the weary walkers. Still, it was better than nothing and more than enough for the *Jacquets* to feel presentable. In any case, it was their souls that they were coming to submit to the benevolence of the Apostle, and these had already been thoroughly cleansed by the Way.

Today, Lavacolla is the location of Santiago de Compostela Airport. Jumbo jets disgorge hordes of pilgrims from around the world, those who found it unnecessary or impossible to come on foot. The airport is so busy that the runway should be extended, or perhaps a new one be built. The Way is dominated by an enormous embankment here, which was barely completed when we passed it. Wire fences, powerful runway lighting, and a tall red and white signal gantry stand right beside the small, wooded ravine through which the pilgrims' path runs.

In the heathlands of Asturias I found the Way imbued with an abstract spirituality, which did not belong to any particular religion and which, for want of a better term, I called Buddhist. But on the approach to Santiago, it is increasingly marked by Christian, or, to be precise, Catholic symbols and values.

At Lavacolla, for example, the Christian virtue of humility comes to the fore. The tiny pilgrim, worn out with fatigue, tramps through the undergrowth, while huge machines – bulldozers, mechanical excavators, trucks – tip out the silty soil that is being used to create the high embankment right beside the Way. Above him roar big gleaming jets that have flown across oceans to get here. The walker feels infinitely small beneath the bellies of these monsters. The tradition that he is honouring and perpetuating with every step seems pathetic, out of touch with today's world and meaningless to all the sensible people who fly to Santiago de Compostela. Yet even so, in a profoundly Christian sense, the tiny, insignificant, trampled soul of the pilgrim is swollen with pride. For he brings to the Apostle something infinitely precious, beyond the reach of airline passengers: his suffering, his time, his efforts, the insignificant and sublime proof of his devotion, the millions of steps taken in all weathers and through the worst terrain, to finally arrive here.

I remember a port in Cantabria, Castro Urdiales, which I reached after a particularly hard week's walking. I had a chat with a French couple whom I met in a restaurant. It turned out that they had come from Hendaye, as I had. The difference – because they were travelling by car – was that they had set off just two hours earlier. This was my first experience of that curious sentiment which inhabits the pilgrim: feeling infinitely small and yet cherishing this humility, to the point where it almost becomes a sin of pride.

After the streams of Lavacolla, the Way rises gently through eucalyptus woods. The next stop on the journey, further away than you might think, is the famous Monte do Gozo. It is called the Mount of Joy because from the summit the red roofs of Santiago de Compostela are visible in the distance.

Without realising it, you start walking faster here, thinking you are about to reach the top. But no, it is still a little bit further. So you carry on, get exhausted and despair. On the way, you daydream and imagine this celebrated summit as an Alpine belvedere, offering a panorama of the landscape stretching off into the horizon. When you finally make one last effort and reach the top of the fabled mountain, soaked in sweat, there is no joy to be had. What you can see is not exactly overwhelming. A gloomy hill, planted with high trees that hide the view. You can just about make out some roofs in the distance, but there are no spectacular views. On the hillside, a huge *albergue*, big enough for the crowds walking along the French Way, is a popular stopover.

At the highest point of Monte do Gozo, a gigantic monument has been erected. There seems to be an unwritten rule that proposals for artistic projects, if submitted to a large number of people, will always result in works that are banal and ugly. Collective decision-making at best produces lukewarm art. You can bet that a great many people were consulted about the statue which crowns Monte do Gozo, for it is difficult to imagine anything more hideous, pretentious or depressing. It could be considered a masterpiece, but only of a very specific genre: Catholic kitsch.

But this thoroughly modern eyesore is not entirely without merit: any pilgrim who had passed the time on the Way dreaming of a return to the Middle Ages and imagining that in this respect Santiago de Compostela would be the apogee of his long journey, will be swiftly brought back to reality. This place is well and truly in the twenty-first century. Santiago is no longer a simple grotto where St James's relics were discovered. It is a modern metropolis, with its unsightly monuments, superstores and motorways. To arrive in Santiago is not a journey back in time but one that takes the pilgrim back to the present, brutally and irrefutably.

Pilgrims on bicycles, whom one encounters here and there on the Way, appear to congregate on the Monte do Gozo, so the walker begins the final descent to the city in the middle of a *peloton*. Although I had always considered bicycles unnecessary if not inappropriate on the Camino, I could see, as I got closer to Santiago, how useful they were, for the route into the city is a Way of Suffering for those on foot. In a place that is supposed to welcome pilgrims, complete priority seems to have been given over to cars, buses, lorries and anything else with an engine.

It is always strange to think that there are people who live in places of pilgrimage all year round. Thinking of Mecca, for example, the picture that comes to our mind is the crowd walking around the Kaaba. If we then look at photos and see apartment buildings with large windows and balconies over-looking the holy place, this seems bizarre, almost incongru-ous. Santiago de Compostela, as we imagine it during the lengthy journey on the Way, comprises simply the Cathedral and the Plaza del Obradoiro in front of it. But as walkers approach the real town, the first things they encounter are VW dealerships, supermarkets and Chinese restaurants. Crowds of locals go about their business, without a thought for the Apostle. Sure, his name is on the signs, but he only seems a local speciality, like nougat from Montélimar or Bêtises de Cambrai. And when you finally walk along the city streets with scallop shells dangling from your rucksack, you feel just as out of place as you have done everywhere else on the journey.

I even wonder if the locals have not had enough of rubbing shoulders with tramps covered in scallop shells. It would be understandable. In any case, they pay them no heed. They do not even appear to see them. This is perhaps the ultimate sign of the arrival: when the walker is still a long way from Santiago, and especially in areas where pilgrims are few, he attracts attention, interest and on occasion sympathy. But when he arrives at Santiago, he is completely invisible. He has simply melted into air.

In the city of the Apostle, the stream of pilgrims is carefully directed along a long path marked with scallop shells, which leads into the old town. It would be an understatement to say it is unwelcoming. But if you manage to avoid being crushed on the dual carriage ring road, or on the intersections, or on the viaducts without pavements, if you succeed in crossing one last circular boulevard without mishap, then the Apostle is definitely watching over you. Then you reach the Puerta del Camino and at last you enter the historic quarter, the centre with all its monuments.

But you should not imagine that you will now savour the unalloyed joy of a poetic journey into the past. A highly contagious disease has spread through these narrow streets. It disfigures like leprosy, defaces the houses, worms its way under the porches and down the side streets. It is the souvenir trade, a very unusual business, for it is devoted to selling objects that are completely useless. Moreover, they also need to be cheap, easy to carry and very ugly. Usually made in China, these knick-knacks take their inspiration from local history, whose symbols are infinitely replicated. It goes without saying that the scallop shell appears *ad nauseam*. It takes the form of brooches, badges, key-rings and mobile phone covers. It decorates table mats, plastic cups, dog collars, baby bibs, doormats and aprons. There is something for everyone.

Pilgrims who have travelled on foot, especially if they have come a long way, feel more alone and more out of place than ever in this tourist trap. For they bear no resemblance to the crowds around them, who may also claim to be followers of the Apostle. The vast majority of these people would be seen as tourists anywhere else but here they call themselves pilgrims. With money in their pockets, they keep the souvenir shops busy. The only way that tourists who come by plane or bus can confirm their ephemeral status of pilgrims is through buying piles of trinkets, proof of their trip to Santiago.

Pilgrims who have walked all the way do not need them because they are the privileged ones: they are entitled to the famous *compostela* certificate, which is formally awarded at the town hall. New arrivals often head straight for the office that issues it.

32

Arrival

The pilgrims reunite in the old building where they obtain their *compostela* certificates. Here, there are no tourists, only authentic *Jacquets*. Some have had time to go to their lodgings and change clothes. Others have come straight from the Way to get in line, their rucksacks still on their backs. This precious document has to be earned, and you have to be patient. Troops of pilgrims hurry to the floor with the counters where the *compostela* is issued. The queue spills out onto the landing, down the stairs and as far as the main entrance – sometimes even into the courtyard. Conversations can be heard in every tongue. At first glance, you can't tell which path each has followed, nor from where they started. But those who have taken unusual routes, such as the Camino de la Plata, usually make this known by giving detailed accounts at the tops of their voices. Those who have come a long way also don't miss any opportunity to share their achievement with whoever is listening. While I was waiting, a young woman a bit further down the stairs kept repeating loudly, "When I left Vézelay . . ."

Despite this, the atmosphere is rather reserved, maybe

because the pilgrims fall into two groups who barely communicate: the walkers and the cyclists. The latter can be recognised by their tight-fitting jerseys. Sometimes they are still wearing their cycling shoes, complete with toe-clips, when they stand at the counters. They are tanned, with shaved arms and legs, and wraparound sunglasses pushed up on their foreheads. When you see one of them next to a ragged and hirsute long-distance walker, it looks as if road-racing champion Chris Froome had bumped into Jean Valjean from *Les Misérables*. But Saint James spreads his cloak of divine mercy over all humanity without distinction. Whether they have come on foot or on two wheels, each leaves with their certificate composed in Latin.

The woman who provides this – it is almost always a woman – unfolds the pilgrim's *credencial*, which is covered with colourful stamps neatly placed in their respective boxes. Only the walker knows what these stamps represent in terms of sweat and toil, cold and hunger. For the office staff, they are devoid of poetry, a mere proof of the journey undertaken, and all they check is whether the candidate has walked at least one hundred kilometres (or cycled a minimum of two hundred). I began to panic for a short moment when the woman told me I had not walked far enough to qualify. I went pale. Eight hundred kilometres! Not enough? But it turned out that she had not completely unfolded the battered accordion of my *credencial*. At last, justice prevailed, and I left the office clutching my certificate.

But once I had obtained the piece of paper I had so dearly

wanted, it suddenly seemed derisory, pointless, even a bit of an encumbrance. How can you slide it into the *mochila* without crumpling it? Finally, I went up to the cathedral square holding it in my hand.

Walking these last few metres ought to be a deeply moving experience. But sadly, circumstances conspire to make it an extremely unpleasant one. A bagpipe player, whose stamina is matched only by his incompetence, usually positions himself in the last covered passageway leading to the cathedral. Just when you want to focus all your thoughts on this final, solemn moment of your pilgrimage, when you have reached the conclusion of your journey, the end of the Way, the shrill squeal of the pipes set your teeth on edge, driving you to distraction like an itch in an awkward spot.

I'd bet that for every ten people who give coins to the piper at least five do so in the secret hope of getting rid of him. But he only takes a break at lunchtime. Torture being most effective when it is continuous, he unfortunately leaves his place to a singer with a guitar, who is an even more hopeless musician, but who at least cannot be heard from quite so far away.

Once you are on the cathedral square, the Plaza del Obradoiro (or Praza do Obradoiro in Gallego), you have reached your journey's end, the kilometre zero of all the routes to Santiago. It is a vast space, surrounded by majestic monuments and dominated by the towering façade of the cathedral. Curiously, although it is the culmination of the Way, it does not seem to belong to it. Day after day, you have come to understand the Way as if it were an old friend. You know it is humble, discreet, a bit confused by the modern world. It doesn't give itself airs, it gently strokes tumbledown old houses as it passes by, and it rushes down steep slopes, bringing a fair bit of mud with it. The Way has no arrogant vanity, only self-respect and dignity; it makes no claims, it forgets nothing. It is a narrow, slight thing that meanders and perseveres, like a human life. But the Plaza del Obradoiro, where it ends, is sumptuous, swollen with power, and built to impress.

I imagine that in the early days of this pilgrimage, at the time of King Alfonso, the journey may have terminated in front of a grotto, or at best a small chapel, just a pile of stones to shelter the saint's relics. At that time, the goal of the Camino must have been as modest as the path itself. Today, though, the Church deploys all the pomp and vanity it can muster at the arrival point. The saint's relics are housed within an incredible sequence of repositories, like the layers of an onion. They are kept in a silver urn, in a crypt which was part of the original ninth-century church on this site. And all this is enclosed in a Gothic cathedral, which in turn is concealed behind a façade built in the eighteenth century. This congregation of art has its own beauty. It provides a framework for the worship of Saint James, a complete choreography. After walking through the nave, visitors descend into the crypt and then go up a stairway to the choir, where they arrive at the back of an immense effigy of Saint James. Tradition requires that each pilgrim gives the saint an *abrazo*, an embrace, a kind of ritual hug from behind. I don't know why, but I couldn't bring myself to do it. It seemed to me that this act of veneration, which was supposed to conclude my journey, would have been a betrayal of its very essence. I had not come to embrace a golden idol, even one sculpted in the image of an Apostle. I may have surrendered myself completely to the many physical initiations that the Way demands of the pilgrim, but I baulked at this last test, even though it was supposed to be a reward. Although I wanted to preserve the concrete meaning that the Way had had for me as I was walking through the valley and villages, I also wanted its culmination to be abstract, symbolic, personal. In short, I had turned the legendary Saint James into a fraternal and philosophical idea that was all my own. I wasn't keen to replace it with the cold touch of a gilded statue worn down by the hands of all those who, claiming to be Catholic, were engaging in a ritual that to me seemed entirely pagan.

I found the pilgrims' High Mass more acceptable, as it was both more traditional and more orthodox. We should stick to the rules of the game: since the Church has appropriated this pilgrimage, which in my opinion is filled with a wider, more abstract spirituality, we should let it provide the finale. Unlike the individual and almost dreamlike gesture of the visitors, who embrace the saint one after the other, the pilgrims' High Mass is a real moment of communion. It is a crucible, which melts together all the differences, the journeys, the ordeals of each pilgrim, to create a beautiful alloy of pure sound for the duration of a prayer.

The cathedral was already packed solid when I arrived. And there was one last cause for irritation: the motorised pilgrims, who had been brought there by their travel agents and whose only effort had been the walk from their hotels, had taken up all the pews. Burdened with their rucksacks, the foot-pilgrims had to stand behind the pillars, next to the side chapels. One day perhaps the last will be first, but during the pilgrims' Mass the social hierarchy is preserved and the down-and-outs are pushed aside.

I managed to squeeze in behind a thick pillar, which blocked my view, but if I twisted round I could just see the choir. Among those standing in the crowd, I spotted several people I had met on the Way, including the man from Haute-Savoie, who had miraculously made it to his destination.

At last, the majestic thunder of the organ filled the cathedral. The great, solemn Mass began, with sermons in various European languages. A nun with the voice of an angel started singing, and the crowd responded in the most wonderful unison.

And then – and I was really lucky here – I witnessed the lighting of the famous Botafumeiro. This enormous thurible, a massive silver cauldron, hangs by a giant chain from the ceiling of the cathedral. When the huge censer filled with myrrh and incense is lit, it gives off as much smoke as a bonfire. Eight men are needed to set it in motion. The thurible swings back and forth in the transept, apparently at a speed of sixty kilometres an hour, filling the whole church with its fragrance. When it started to swing, a nun intoned the first words of a hymn and the crowd joined in with enthusiasm. This spectacular ceremony has been perfected over the course of centuries and is intensely moving. When the Botafumeiro is returned to its place and the last notes of the hymn are sung, the congregation is suddenly left exhausted, drained of emotion, happy to have shared this special moment. This is truly the end of the pilgrimage.

An Italian, with whom I chatted as we were left the cathedral, told me a detail that could have broken the spell. According to him, the ritual of the Botafumeiro was originally not so much religious as sanitary. In the Middle Ages the pilgrims, despite passing through Lavacolla, were so filthy that when the cathedral was packed with these unwashed bodies, the air was literally unbreathable. If the priests were to survive, the only solution was to swing a barrel of incense in the air. But far from putting me off the ceremony, his anecdote helped me reconcile two contrasting realities hitherto incompatible: the splendour of the Christian liturgy and the primitive simplicity of the Way. Thus incense and magnificence were united with sweat and mud. The thread was unbroken.

Everything conspires to break it, though, once you have

'arrived'. The charm and beauty of Santiago de Compostela can bury your memories of the Way. The body gets back into urban mode: you idly wander in the narrow streets and before long you'll even find yourself buying souvenirs . . .

And then an aircraft lifts you out of this holy place and in a few short hours brings you back to your familiar surroundings. When you were walking along the Camino, you used to tell yourself that you would never drive a car again without thinking about those making the same journey on foot. But as soon as you are behind the wheel, you forget all these resolutions and speed off without a second thought.

Some lessons of the Way are not so quickly forgotten. In my case, this was especially true of the philosophy of the mochila. For several months after my return, I tried to apply my reflections on my fears to the whole of my life. I calmly examined what I carried on my back. I cast off many things, many projects, many constraints. I tried to lighten my load to make it easier to bear the mochila of existence.

But that, too, passed. The page gradually turned and the anxieties of the Way disappeared. The perceptible effects of the pilgrimage soon fade. After a few weeks, it's all gone. Life returns to normal. Nothing seems to have changed.

Of course there are signs that suggest that my pilgrimage is still having an impact, somewhere deep down. It is certainly not a coincidence that I began to work on a history of the fifteenth-century merchant Jacques Cœur after I had returned.

The house of his birth is beside one of the routes to Santiago, and as a child he watched the *Jacquets* pass by. He felt the ardent desire to make the pilgrimage himself, but circumstances denied him the opportunity. Following his life, along the paths of the Middle Ages, I felt a bit as if I had once again picked up my *mochila* and set off on a new journey, this time through writing. Jacques Cœur, like the pilgrims, found freedom when he lost everything. And he did have everything – money, power, luxury – so his radical sacrifice gave his destiny a nobility that is not foreign to the spirit of the Way.

But all this was just an indirect, vague influence for me. The pilgrimage itself soon became no more than a distant memory. I felt that its philosophical essence, which I had gathered drop by drop as I was writing *Le Grand Cœur*, had been extracted by squeezing out all the special moments of the journey. All that remained of the Way was some essential lesson, and a rather vague one at that. It is intoxicating and precious, but hard to define. I thought I had forgotten everything.

Then, one snowy day in Chamonix, I told two friends about the pilgrimage over lunch. Marie-Christine Guérin and Christophe Raylat, who run the publishing house Éditions Guérin, are very keen mountaineers. They were interested to hear about my journey and asked me lots of questions, just as they would ask other mountaineers who had come back from an expedition. So I shared a few anecdotes with them, remembered things I'd forgotten. It was just one of those conversations between climbers that a glass of white wine and the warmth of the chalet can stimulate, particularly if it is freezing outside. When at the end of the meal my friends encouraged me to turn these memories into a book, I was quite indignant. I had not gone on this pilgrimage to write about the experience! Indeed, I hadn't written a word, either during the journey or when I got back. I had wanted to experience it in the present, without having to step back and explain it, even to myself. And when I saw pilgrims feverishly making notes in the evenings, I used to feel sorry for them.

But then, as I walked home across a white landscape on this bitterly cold winter's day, images started coming back to me, of brilliant blue skies and muddy paths, lonely *ermitas*, and coasts battered by Atlantic waves. In the prison of memory, the Way was stirring, knocking on the walls, and calling me. I began to think, and I began to write, and when I picked up the thread, it all came back.

Nothing had been lost. It is wrong, or just too easy, to think that a journey like this one is simply a journey and nothing more, to be forgotten and put away in a box. I would not be able to explain the workings of the Way, nor what it truly represents. I only know that it is alive and that you cannot say anything about it except everything, as I have tried to do in this book. But even then the essential part is missing, and I know it. That is why, sometime soon, I'll set off again.

And so will you.

JEAN-CHRISTOPHE RUFIN is a doctor, diplomat, historian, globetrotter and novelist. He is the president of Action Against Hunger, one of the founders of Médecins Sans Frontières and was the second youngest member of the Académie française. He was Ambassador of France in Senegal from 2007 to June 2010. His novel *Brazil Red* won the Prix Goncourt in 2007.

MARTINA DERVIS and MALCOLM IMRIE are London-based editors and translators. Between them, they have translated some thirty books. They often work together, and this is their third joint translation from French.